First released 2018
Reprinted 2019

Published by:

Inspirations Studios Corpration Pty Ltd

PO Box 10177
Adelaide Business Hub
South Australia 5000
Australia

www.inspirationsstudios.com

Editor: Susan O'Connor

Assistant Editor: Ellaine Bronsert

Graphic Design: Lynton Grandison

Photographic Styling:
Fiona Fagan & Natalie Homan

Photography: Brendan Homan

Production Manager: Jessie Huber

Kit Manager: Sue Forrest

Studio Management:
Kristian & Andrea Fleming

Inspirations –
A Passion for Needlework
Factoria VII
ISBN 978 0 6482873 1 5

© Copyright 2018
Inspirations Studios Corporation Pty Ltd

INSPIRATIONS
a passion for needlework

Factoria VII

NEEDLEWORK.

It draws you in with luscious silks, beguiling ribbons and
shimmering beads.

Needles glide with precision, threads dance – yielding to the skill of
the hand.

The rhythm of the stitch soothes your senses, lifts your spirit,
nourishes your soul and ignites your passion.

It calls to us. It compels us to stitch... and stitch we do.

We stitch our stories, we stitch our love, we stitch our pain, we stitch
our dreams. We stitch and it makes the world more beautiful.

Needlework – such a magnificent pursuit.

IT BEGAN BY ASKING THE QUESTION, 'WHAT IF?'

What if there was a book almost as beautiful as needlework itself.
What if each project was an adventure, telling its own bespoke story.

'A Passion for Needlework' by Inspirations was created in 2016 to
showcase needlework unlike anything before. Evocative. Lush. Bold.

Now the adventure continues...

'A Passion for Needlework | Factoria VII' brings to life twelve brand
new masterpieces in a singular spectacular setting. Twelve unique and
individual stories, one unified aesthetic.

The world's most beautiful never rests, it's always on the move and now
a new journey awaits with more passion, more wonder and more beauty
longing to be discovered.

Join us... it won't be the same without you.

contents

Hidden

Raw beauty is often hidden. To find it, one requires a keen eye and patience.

Factoria VII is an extraordinarily unique cottage hidden away in the backblocks of the Adelaide Hills in the tiny rural township of Dawesley, South Australia. Most locals have never heard of Dawesley; it now has no services, no post office, just a cluster of homes – the perfect place for something to be hidden.

The beauty of Factoria VII has been over a century in the making. With no trace remaining of its original purpose other than its documented history, this rustic, industrial house is the perfect backdrop to showcase some of the world's most beautiful needlework. A role that is a far cry from its origins.

History

In 1857 the Adelaide Hills were abuzz with the establishment of new mines and smelters thanks, in part, to the recent discovery of copper. This gave William Bower Dawes good reason to believe the nearby allotments he was selling in his newly laid town of Dawesley 'will become very valuable'. By the 1860s, Dawesley would be home to over a dozen residences and three industrial buildings: a post office/general store, a school and a bacon factory.

The district flourished and became a significant copper mining area with the town of Dawesley playing its intended role of providing services and accommodation for the smelters. The hero of our story however, is the bacon factory which would survive long after the rattle and hum of the mines were silenced, eventually becoming known as Factoria VII.

Established in 1877 by Mr Elias Davies, the 'Davies Bacon Factory' was instrumental in the early growth and economic development of Dawesley, offering meat processing for farmers, boosting the local livestock industry and supplying small goods to the mining community. Processing roughly 25 pigs per week, the animals were sourced locally or transported in by rail, then cured into bacon with the cuttings and trimmings made into sausages and lard.

Over time, as the local mineral deposits dried up, the mines were shuttered, local industry declined, people moved away and in 1943 the Dawesley school closed its doors for the last time. Through it all the bacon factory remained standing and was soon to enter a new era.

Conversion

In the 1980s an architect purchased the factory and took on the challenge of converting this now historic landmark from a bacon processing facility into a family home. Huge reclaimed wharf timbers were trucked in and installed throughout as the original two-storey barn became a spacious living area downstairs, with three bedrooms, a loft and a bathroom upstairs. To complete the makeover, in the heart of the home, a large, open country-style kitchen was created featuring a large dining area, a cosy combustion fire and French doors overlooking the outdoor courtyard.

Transformation

During 2010, the property changed hands and new owners ushered in a new chapter of the story. The heavy wood from the substantial beams stained in dark colours typical of the 80s, and the original unsealed and dusty stone walls were earmarked for transformation. In place of the original earthy tones, a vision for a simple, bright-white interior was brought to life. Nothing escaped the white revolution which, once completed, gave rise to a more modern, light filled and visually expansive living space. With everything now awash in uniform white, all the complex textures and striking lines of the original industrial design and characteristics of the mid-19th Century pioneering construction techniques, were accentuated to great effect.

Decorated with a personal collection of beautiful vintage, handmade and natural furnishings, blending perfectly with the textural and tactile feel of the home, the current owners have created a spectacular space. To truly make it their own the Davies Bacon Factory was renamed 'Factoria VII', speaking simultaneously to its new future and as homage to its industrial heritage.

Collision

One does not typically associate rough stone walls, scarred by maker and time with the delicate intricacies of fine, hand-stitched reticella. Nor weathered, reclaimed wharf timbers with precise goldwork or detailed silk embroidery. Yet the juxtaposition of the flawed alongside the perfect, the pristine befriending the tarnished is what A Passion for Needlework Factoria VII celebrates.

All at once it creates familiarity and tension – it's what you expect, but not where you expect it.

A collision of two beautiful worlds ensues – one to serve as backdrop to the other.

One texture-rich, stone and wood cottage.

Twelve extraordinary needlework projects.

Take up your needle and thread – a new adventure begins...

gallery

flower pots

BY ANA MALLAH OF AUSTRALIA

The Flower

Once in a golden hour
I cast to earth a seed.
Up there came a flower,
The people said, a weed.

To and fro they went
Thro' my garden bower,
And muttering discontent
Cursed me and my flower.

Then it grew so tall
It wore a crown of light,
But thieves from o'er the wall
Stole the seed by night.

Sow'd it far and wide
By every town and tower,
Till all the people cried,
'Splendid is the flower!'

Read my little fable:
He that runs may read.
Most can raise the flowers now,
For all have got the seed.

And some are pretty enough,
And some are poor indeed;
And now again the people
Call it but a weed.

Alfred, Lord Tennyson (1809-1892)

Exquisite stumpwork flowers sit atop these
sweet little embroidered pots. More than
eighty petals in shades of pink, blue, green
and violet are arranged to create a lavish
bouquet of hydrangeas. Lush pink open
blooms and buds are surrounded with leaves
and a tiny ladybird rests among the petals
on the rose pot.

jacobean hunt

BY PHILLIPA TURNBULL OF THE UK

Hunting has been practiced in England since prehistoric times when survival depended on obtaining meat for food and skins for clothing and shelter. Hunting with hounds was popular during the Iron Age (800BC-43AD) and when the Romans conquered Britain (43AD) they brought with them new breeds of hunting dogs and new prey such as the fallow deer and brown hare. With advances in agriculture and farming, by the Jacobean period (1567-1625), deer hunting had changed from a necessity for survival to a pleasure pursuit for the aristocracy. Strict laws prevented commoners from taking game from private lands or royal estates and, despite the penalties, poaching was commonplace and gamekeepers were kept busy protecting game while eliminating poachers and vermin. Large lodges were built on vast, wooded estates and hunting parties became the preferred sport of royalty. The enjoyment of the quest was enhanced by providing meat for the banquet table and competition was fierce to hunt a stag with large antlers as the ultimate reward.

A wonderful reinterpretation of a 17th century design, this crewel embroidery depicts a deer hunt in a fantastic forest, worked in a rich palette of woollen threads on a linen twill background. Oversized flowers, oak and grapes surround a colourful bird in the upper section while the pursuit takes place along the lower edge.

red currants

BY JULIE KNIEDL OF AUSTRALIA

R*ibes rubrum, is native across Western Europe and a member of the gooseberry family. A deciduous shrub growing to 1.5m (5'), the red currant has insignificant, cupped yellow flowers that develop into very attractive, glossy, red spheres that hang in racemes of three to ten fruits. Mature berries are tart but sweet and can be eaten raw or made into jellies and jams, often to accompany roast meats, and used in fruit soups and summer puddings. Red currants are the most common filling for the famous Linzer torte from Linz, Austria.*

Loved by gourmets worldwide, Bar-Le-Duc, or Lorraine jelly originated from Bar-Le-Duc, Lorraine, France and can be made from red or white currants. To prepare the berries, the seeds must be painstakingly removed by hand, traditionally using a finely tapered goose quill to open a small flap in the skin, lift out the seeds and carefully close the opening.

Once prepared, the berries are weighed and an equal weight of sugar and some water are placed in a saucepan and heated. The berries are added for several minutes then removed, keeping them intact. The syrup is slowly simmered until thickened then poured over the fruit and sealed into jars. Made since the 1300s, honey was originally used and the resulting conserve is traditionally eaten with toast and sweet butter, madeleines or vanilla ice-cream.

Wooden beads, wire and wool threads are used to create this spectacular, three-dimensional stem of vibrant red currants. Luscious globes of gleaming red are offset by fresh green leaves and a rich brown wooden stem.

le magnolia

BY CATHERINE LAURENÇON OF FRANCE

Magnolia x soulangeana, the saucer magnolia, has an open, spreading habit and is regarded as one of the best specimen trees for home gardens. Hybridised from *Magnolia denudata* and *Magnolia liliiflora*, it has its origins in Fromont, France where it was developed by Étienne Soulange-Bodin, a retired cavalry officer in Napoleon's army, and first flowered in 1826. The beautiful, white, pink or violet flowers are highly scented and appear on the naked branches in early to mid-spring and can measure up to 20cm (8") across. They are followed by glossy, dark green leaves and red fruits that are very attractive to birds.

Magnolia is a large, ancient genus of more than two hundred flowering plant species and is named after the French botanist Pierre Magnol. The superb, fragrant flowers display tepals rather than petals, a combination of petal and sepal that is initially enclosed within a bract and an indicator of the extreme age of the species.

Stitched onto pure white linen, this threadpainted study captures the elegant beauty of the spectacular saucer magnolia. Numerous shades of pink, purple and soft green stranded cotton combine to give form to the striking cupped tepals of this stunning flower.

versailles chatelaine

BY SUSAN O'CONNOR OF AUSTRALIA

Originally built in 1624 as a hunting lodge by Louis Xlll, the Palace of Versailles was enlarged in several stages to create the magnificent chateau with two thousand, three hundred rooms that stands today. The first phase of expansion was carried out by Louis XIV and occurred between 1661 and 1678, involving significant building and landscaping work with the addition of three stone wings that were lavishly finished and decorated by the best French craftsmen. The buildings were surrounded by superb gardens with spectacular fountains and countless statues. Between 1678 and 1715 two massive wings were added and alterations were made to the existing building that led to Louis XIV proclaiming the palace his principal residence and moving the seat of government to Versailles in 1682 where it remained until the French Revolution. In 1789 Louis XVI was forced to leave the palace for Paris, ending its role as a royal residence. In 1837 Versailles became the Museum of the History of France and today it is one of the most visited sites in the country, stunning visitors with its magnificence and opulent decoration.

Stripes and florals are frequently
paired in traditional French textiles,
the sensuous curves of flower petals
contrasting beautifully with formal
lines. This elegant chatelaine includes
a pinwheel, scissor sheath with fob and
needlebook with a monogrammed cover.
Stitched onto ivory silk with silk threads,
the trellis stripes divide rows of sweet
bullion rose bouquets in shades of pink,
soft blue and violet.

reticella sampler

BY CHRISTINE P. BISHOP OF AUSTRALIA

Reticella is Italian for 'a small net' and is a form of needlelace also known as reticello and point coupé or point coupe in French.

Dating from the 15th century, this technique was originally a form of cutwork in which threads were removed, horizontally and vertically, from the linen ground fabric leaving a grid over which a pattern was stitched. The edges of the cut areas were reinforced and diagonal threads were laid in to stabilise the open spaces. Designs were characteristically geometric with squares, rectangles and circles further embellished with arches and scallops. As the open areas became larger, additional temporary threads were needed to support the ground fabric and eventually the fabric was removed completely and the reticella was worked over a grid of unattached threads, becoming a true form of needlelace. Worked with linen thread, the resulting lace was used to create ornate collars, cuffs and edging for ruffs and spectacular examples can be seen in English and European portraits from the 16th and 17th centuries.

The elaborate patterns of reticella, worked as a line sampler, create a superb lacy surface, enhanced by the single colour of the fabric and thread. Worked in rows of increasing intricacy, each line builds on the techniques of the one above.

winter sunset

BY HAZEL BLOMKAMP OF SOUTH AFRICA

A Sunset

I love the evenings, passionless and fair, I love the evens,
Whether old manor-fronts their ray with golden fulgence leavens,
In numerous leafage bosomed close;
Whether the mist in reefs of fire extend its reaches sheer,
Or a hundred sunbeams splinter in an azure atmosphere
On cloudy archipelagos.

Oh, gaze ye on the firmament! a hundred clouds in motion,
Up-piled in the immense sublime beneath the winds' commotion,
Their unimagined shapes accord:
Under their waves at intervals flame a pale levin through,
As if some giant of the air amid the vapors drew
A sudden elemental sword.

The sun at bay with splendid thrusts still keeps the sullen fold;
And momently at distance sets, as a cupola of gold,
The thatched roof of a cot a-glance;
Or on the blurred horizon joins his battle with the haze;
Or pools the blooming fields about with inter-isolate blaze,
Great moveless meres of radiance.

Victor Hugo (1802-1885)

A magical palette of gentle
pastels and intricate stitch techniques
creates a fascinating surface on this
square footstool. Fabulous Jacobean
flowers are filled with composite
stitching, weaving and threadpainting
then further enhanced with the velvet
tufts of Ghiordes knots.

leaping hare

BY BARBARA KERSHAW OF CANADA

C asalguidi, or punto Casale, is a unique style of embroidery named for a charming village in the Tuscan countryside, northwest of Florence. Using a monochromatic palette and neutral colours, the embroidery is characterized by light, open backgrounds worked using pulled or withdrawn thread stitches and robust, high-relief motifs fashioned from needlelace and padded, detached stitch techniques. Elegant geometric forms are often combined with flowers, fruit and leaves, real and imagined animals and human figures plus the distinctive six-petalled rosettes and characteristic stick or 'bastone' motif that are easy identifiers of this style. Small bags and sachets are a traditional vehicle for this style of embroidery, stitched onto evenweave linen and often finished with charming, hand-made tassels and cords, the size and purpose perfect to showcase the sculptural quality of the stitching.

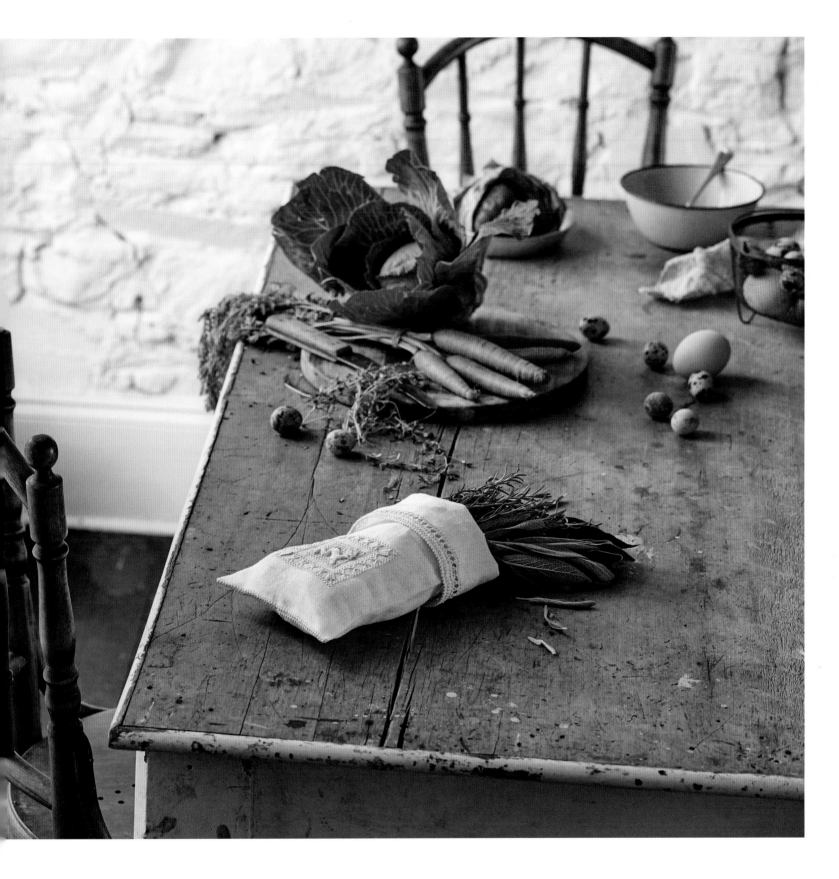

A graceful, high-relief hare leaps across a background
of four-sided stitch on this charming linen sachet.
Worked using monochromatic fabric and thread, the sachet
is finished with a decorative edge and twisted cords.

edinburgh etui

BY BETSY MORGAN OF THE USA

"I am myself a Queen, the daughter of a King, a stranger, and the true Kinswoman of the Queen of England. I came to England on my cousin's promise of assistance against my enemies and rebel subjects and was at once imprisoned... As an absolute Queen, I cannot submit to orders, nor can I submit to the laws of the land without injury to myself, the King my son and all other sovereign princes... For myself I do not recognize the laws of England nor do I know or understand them as I have often asserted. I am alone without counsel, or anyone to speak on my behalf. My papers and notes have been taken from me, so that I am destitute of all aid, taken at a disadvantage."

Mary, Queen of Scots
On trial for plotting to assassinate her cousin,
Elizabeth I, Queen of England and Ireland in 1586
Executed February 8th 1587

The eglantine rose of England, thistle of Scotland and shamrock of Ireland represent the domains at the heart of the conflict between Elizabeth I and Mary Queen of Scots in the 16th Century. Stitched with counted and surface embroidery techniques, this delightful etui includes a thimble case, needlebook, scissor fob and pincushion.

the linnet

BY NICOLA JARVIS OF THE UK

The Linnet

Upon this leafy bush
With thorns and roses in it,
Flutters a thing of light,
A twittering linnet.
And all the throbbing world
Of dew and sun and air
By this small parcel of life
Is made more fair;
As if each bramble-spray
And mounded gold-wreathed furze,
Harebell and little thyme,
Were only hers;
As if this beauty and grace
Did to one bird belong,
And, at a flutter of wing,
Might vanish in song.

Walter de la Mare (1873-1956)

Sparkling metal and lustrous silk threads, fabric, sequins and beads fashion the plumage of this graceful linnet. Held within a gilded cage, the contrasting surfaces of polychrome thread embroidery and metal thread work create a spectacular and endearing image.

blackwell roundel

BY JENNY ADIN-CHRISTIE OF THE UK

Built between 1898 and 1900, Blackwell is a captivating historic house overlooking Lake Windermere in the Lake District, Cumbria. Designed by architect MH Baillie Scott for Sir Edward Holt, brewery owner and Lord Mayor of Manchester, the building is regarded as a masterpiece of twentieth-century design and a perfect example of the Arts and Crafts Movement. Built from local slate and sandstone, the house is asymmetrical in design featuring a series of gables that add complexity to the roof line. Most of the original decorative features remain intact and include magnificent plasterwork, superb carved panelling, stained glass, fireplace inglenooks and ornamental window catches and door handles. Many of the leading designers and studios of the Arts and Crafts Movement produced the furniture and objects that fill the rooms including pieces by Morris & Co, Ruskin Pottery, William de Morgan and Stanley Webb Davies.

Open to the public since 2001, the house hosts regular exhibitions and is surrounded by terraced gardens with fragrant flowers, herbs, and sweeping lawn.

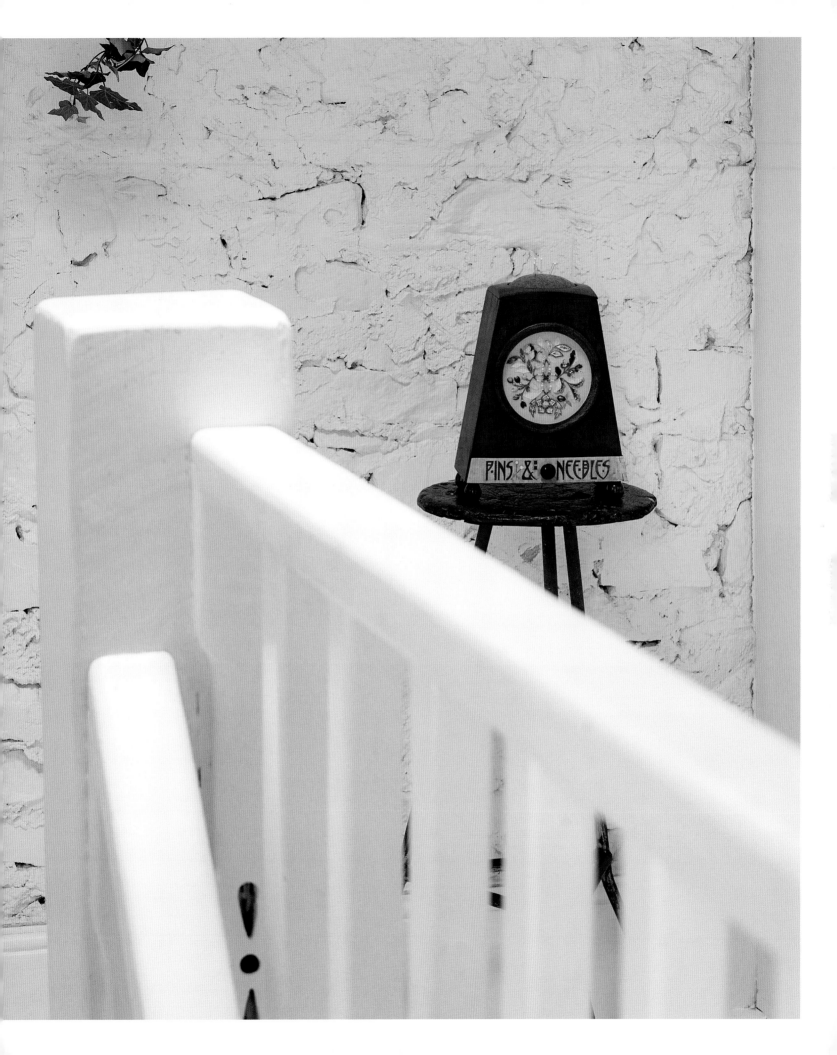

Inspired by the rich decoration
in the white drawing room of
Blackwell, this superb design of
stylised flowers, leaves, fruit and
berries utilises surface embroidery
and goldwork techniques. Echoing
the colours of the room, the roundel is
worked in rich browns and golds on an
ivory organza background.

bee-eaters

BY RENETTE KUMM OF SOUTH AFRICA

The European bee-eater (Merops apiaster) is a beautiful bird with breeding plumage of gold, chestnut, blue, white and black. Both males and females share the spectacular colouring with the females often easily distinguished by a green back. Typically monogamous, a breeding pair will excavate a metre long nesting burrow in an earth or sand bank. The long tunnel terminates in a nest chamber where the female will lay between four and seven eggs. After hatching, the chicks are fed by the parents and sometimes, 'helpers-at-the-nest', either sons of the breeding pair or brothers of the breeding male who have failed in their own breeding attempts. Bee-eaters are one of the few European species who follow this practice. As indicated by their name, the birds feed on honey bees and a wide variety of other insects, especially dragonflies. On catching prey, the bird returns to its perch and strikes the insect's head to kill it and with bees, wipes the abdomen against the perch to release the sting.

With a range spanning 11 million square kilometres, the bee-eater breeds in Europe, Africa and southern-central Asia and most of the population migrates to sub-Saharan Africa for the winter.

A pair of striking European bee-eaters rest on a leafy branch in this glorious study. Worked with lustrous silk threads onto cotton sateen, the glowing colours and precise detailing create an amazingly lifelike rendition of this beautiful bird.

instructions

flower pots

before you begin

We recommend that you read the complete article and instructions in the liftout pattern

See the liftout pattern for the templates

All embroidery is worked with ONE strand of thread unless specified

this design uses

Blanket stitch / Couching
French knot
Long and short blanket stitch
Long and short stitch
Overcasting / Satin stitch
Split stitch / Straight stitch
Wrapping

The hydrangea barrel measures 7cm x 9cm in diameter (2¾" x 3½") and the rose pot measures 8.5cm x 7.5cm in diameter (3⅜" x 3")

HYDRANGEA BARREL

requirements

FABRIC
40cm (16") square of quilter's muslin
20cm x 30cm wide (8" x 12") piece of green spot cotton
35cm (14") square of brown cotton homespun (to match brown felt)

SUPPLIES
20cm x 40cm wide (8" x 16") piece of olive green wool felt
10cm (4") square of brown wool felt

4.5cm x 25cm wide (1¾" x 10") piece of white wool felt
4.5cm x 26cm wide (1¾" x 10¼") piece of thin wadding
15cm (6") embroidery hoop
30cm (12") embroidery hoop
22 x 31cm (12") lengths of 26 gauge white paper-covered wire
30cm x 9mm wide (12" x ⅜") dark brown ribbon
29.5cm x 21cm (A4) piece of firm card
29.5cm x 21cm (A4) piece of template plastic
Copic markers to match thread colours (optional)
Ruler
Fibre-fill
Clear craft glue
Acid-free gluestick
Wire cutters
Tracing paper
Fine black pen
Heat-soluble fabric marker
Sharp HB pencil

NEEDLES
No. 16 chenille
No. 20 chenille
No. 8 crewel

THREADS & BEADS
Anchor stranded cotton
A = 268 vy dk avocado

Cosmo stranded cotton
B = 116 ultra lt pine green
C = 324 vy lt avocado
D = 2323 ultra lt avocado

Cottage Garden Threads stranded cotton
E = 208 lettuce leaf

DMC no. 5 perlé cotton
F = 612 med taupe
G = 3013 lt khaki green

DMC stranded cotton
H = 611 dk taupe
I = 734 lt olive green
J = 839 chocolate
K = 3733 dusky rose

Gumnut Yarns Stars stranded silk
L = 074 carnation

Threadworx variegated stranded cotton
M = 1015 ice blue
N = 1033 ice tea
O = 1103 pretty n' pink
P = 1125 arboretum
Q = 1135 spring time

Sewing thread
R = ivory

Mill Hill no. 11 seed beads
S = 03026 wild blueberry (7)
T = 03058 mardi gras red (13)

preparation for embroidery

PREPARING THE FABRICS

Cut the piece of quilters muslin into four, 20cm (8") squares.

From the white felt, cut twenty, 4.5cm x 1cm wide (1¾" x ⅜") strips. Use the stave template to shape the ends of each piece.

Cut one 4.5cm x 26cm wide (1¾" x 10⅜") strip from the firm card and template plastic. With the edges aligned with the straight grain, centre the card strip on the brown homespun and trace around the shape with the heat-soluble fabric marker. On the wrong side of the homespun, position the strip of thin wadding within the marked lines and tack in place. Centre the homespun into the 30cm (12") hoop and tension until taut, taking care to ensure that the lines are not distorted.

Cut the piece of olive green wool felt into two, 5cm x 24cm wide (2" x 9½") strips, two, 10cm (4") squares and one, 15cm (6") square.

TRANSFERRING THE DESIGN

Centre the inner ring of the 15cm (6") hoop on one piece of quilter's muslin. Using the heat-soluble fabric marker, trace around the inside of the inner ring. Repeat on the remaining three squares. Trace the petal templates and three leaf templates onto the tracing paper using the black pen. Using a lightbox or window and working within the marked circles, trace the three leaves onto one piece of fabric and the eighty-two petals, evenly distributed between the remaining three pieces of fabric and any remaining space on the leaf fabric using the heat-soluble fabric marker. Place one of the pieces of fabric with petal shapes into the 15cm (6") hoop and tension until taut.

embroidery

See page 88 for step-by-step instructions for working a hydrangea petal.

Refer to the close-up photograph for colour placement.

Use the no. 20 chenille needle for the perlé thread, the no. 16 chenille for inserting the wires and the no. 8 crewel needle for all embroidery.

All embroidery is worked in a hoop.

ORDER OF WORK

PETALS

All petals are stitched in the same manner. Work eleven petals each of **E** and **P** and twelve petals each of **L**, **M**, **N**, **O** and **Q**.

For each petal, cut a 7.5cm (3") length of wire. Fold the length of wire in half. Position the fold at the tip of the petal and mould the wire to fit the shape. Alternatively, after folding the wire in half, mould it around a pen or pencil to create the petal shape. Work the petals following the step-by-step instructions.

LEAVES

For each leaf cut an 8cm (3⅛") length of wire. Beginning 5mm (³⁄₁₆") from the tip

on the centre vein, couch the wire down the vein using two strands of **B** (diag 1).

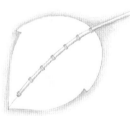

Using the same thread, overcast the wire along the vein.

Using **B**, bring the thread to the surface at the tip end of the wire. Work a detached chain from the end of the wire to the tip of the leaf but do not anchor the stitch. Pull the thread firmly so that the two sides lie together (diag 2).

Work long and short blanket stitch down one side of the leaf, initially working to the vein then, as the leaf widens, to approximately halfway into the leaf (diag 3).

Fill the remaining area with long and short stitch beginning with **C** and finishing with **A**. Work the second side of the leaf and the remaining leaves in the same manner. Using **R**, stitch the leaf veins with long split stitches.

Once all petals and leaves are complete, remove the fabric from the hoop and carefully cut out using sharp embroidery scissors. Angle the blades beneath the beaded edge of the blanket stitch to obtain a clean, close cut.

If desired, colour the cut edge of the fabric with the *Copic* markers.

BARREL

Staves

Beginning on the left-hand side of the shape, position a piece of white felt onto the brown homespun in the hoop, aligning the left long edge and upper and lower edges with the lines. Using **F**, hold the felt in place with several small stab stitches around the edge. Using the same thread, cover the felt with satin stitch. Work random straight stitches over the satin stitch using two strands of **H** (diag 4).

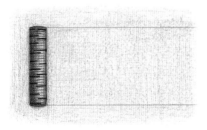

Lay a second strip next to the first and stitch in the same manner. Using two strands of **J**, work a line of split stitch between the staves. Continue adding and stitching strips and working the lines of split stitch. Once all the strips are attached there should be approximately 2cm (¾") uncovered at the right-hand end of the shape (diag 5).

Remove the fabric from the hoop and cut out the shape leaving a 2.5cm (1") seam allowance. Place on a flat surface, wrong side uppermost. Apply a thin layer of craft glue to one side of the strip of firm card. Press the card strip, glue side down, to the back of the embroidered shape. Allow to dry.

Apply a thin layer of craft glue to the wrong side of the seam allowance on each end of the fabric. Fold in, over the card, and press in place. Repeat on the upper and lower edges. Allow to dry.

Hoop

Apply a thin line of craft glue along the length of the wrong side of the ribbon. Leaving a 1cm (⅜") extension at the left-hand end, centre the ribbon over the staves and press in place. Trim away the excess from the right-hand end. Fold the extension to the wrong side and press in place. Allow to dry.

CONSTRUCTING THE BARREL

Sides

At the right-hand end of the strip, apply a thin layer of craft glue to the uncovered fabric. Curve the left-hand end of the strip around and press in place over the glued area to form the barrel sides (diag 6).

Hold in place with clips or pegs until the glue is dry.

Lining

Slide the strip of template plastic down inside and adjust so that it sits firmly against the sides. Mark the upper edge of the plastic where it overlaps. Remove and trim so that it fits exactly without any overlap. Centre and glue one strip of green felt to one side of the plastic, trimming the short felt ends only if it is too long. Secure a 70cm (28") length of **F** to the inner top edge of the barrel sides. Slide the felt covered plastic strip, felt side innermost, down inside the barrel sides. Work blanket stitch, with the stitches 5mm (³⁄₁₆") apart to secure the top edge of the felt to the upper edge of the barrel. Repeat at the remaining long edge of the barrel.

Base

Using the base template, cut one from the firm card and one from the template plastic to create the base circle. Glue the two circles together and allow to dry. Trace the template onto one 10cm (4") square each of brown and olive green felt. Cut out the olive green felt slightly smaller than the outline and the brown felt slightly larger than the outline. Apply a thin layer of craft glue to the plastic side of the base circle and centre, glue side down, on the brown felt. Press firmly and allow to dry. Repeat with the card side of the circle and the olive green felt (diag 7).

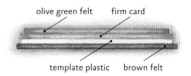

olive green felt   firm card

template plastic   brown felt

With the brown felt outermost and using **F**, stitch the base to one end of the barrel with blanket stitch in the same manner as before.

PREPARING THE LID

Trace the lid template onto the 15cm (6") square of olive green felt. Using the heat-soluble marker, measure in 1cm (⅜") from the marked line and mark a second circle. The majority of the petals will be applied within this line. Cut out the felt circle along the outer line.

Attaching the petals and leaves

Put seventeen petals aside for later use.

Begin on one side of the circle with the pink petals. Take the no. 16 chenille needle through the felt approximately 1cm (⅜") in from the second line, leaving half of the eye above the surface. Feed the wires from the first petal through the eye to the wrong side. Gently pull the needle through the felt and remove. Pull the wires through until the base of the petal is sitting on the felt surface. Bend the wires back behind the petal and, using **I**, stitch to the felt for 5mm

(³⁄₁₆"). Bend the wires back on themselves and stitch in place. Trim away any excess wire. Repeat with three more petals, leaving a small space at the centre to create the first flower. Before adding any additional flowers the leaves should be positioned evenly around the circle with the base of each one approximately 1cm (⅜") in from the second line. Once applied, the majority of each leaf will extend beyond the line. Position the first leaf so that the base is overlapped by the petals of the flower (diag 8).

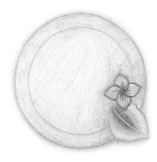

Attach the single wire of each leaf in the same manner as the petals. Excluding the green petals, attach each colour in a cluster before moving on to the next.

NOTE: Not all flowers need to have four petals. As the circle begins to fill add three and two petal flowers to fit the available space.

Intersperse the green petals across the circle. Attach an **S** bead at the centre of each blue and purple flower and an **R** bead at the centre of each pink and green flower using **K**.

Refer to the lift-out pattern for forming the lid base and attaching the upper lid.

Attaching the edge petals

The edge petals are added to the upper lid as eight pairs and one single petal. On the wrong side of each petal secure a length of **I** at the base. Wrap the wire for approximately 1cm (⅜") and secure the thread to the wire with the gluestick. Place two petals together and, using both threads, continue wrapping the wire for 1.5cm (⅝") (diag 9).

Secure the threads to the wire with the gluestick and once dry, trim away the excess wire and threads.

Secure a length of **I** at the base and wrap the wire of the single petal for 2cm (¾") and secure the thread to the wire with the gluestick. Once dry, trim away the excess thread and wire.

To attach the petals, secure a length of **I** beneath an overlapping petal or leaf. Beginning at this point with the end of the stem, couch each stem in place. Repeat for the remaining pairs and single petal ensuring that all stem ends are concealed beneath overlapping petals or leaves.

Finishing

Place the lid on the barrel and, using the end of a chopstick or knitting needle, shape the petals and leaves.

constructing the lid

See the liftout pattern.

HYDRANGEA PETAL

Couch the wire and work the main petal embroidery using **E, L, M, N, O, P** or **Q**.
To begin, fold the wire in half and position the fold at the petal tip.

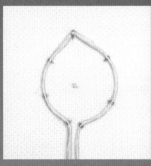

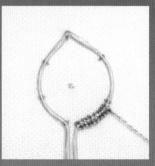

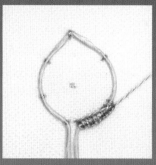

1 | Secure the thread within the petal with two small back stitches. Couch the wire in place around the petal.

2 | Beginning at the base at the right-hand side, work eight close blanket stitches over the wire.

3 | To work the next blanket stitch, take the thread to the back at the base of the petal and complete the stitch.

4 | Begin working long and short blanket stitches around the petal, angling the stitches towards the base.

5 | Continue around the petal until the shape is completely covered.

6 | Cover the remaining wire with close blanket stitches in the same manner as the first eight stitches.

7 | If desired, work several straight stitches in another petal colour to create variation.

8 | Using **J**, work three straight stitches into the base of the petal.

requirements

FABRIC

40cm (16") square of quilter's muslin

30cm (12") square of olive green homespun (to match felt)

SUPPLIES

25cm (10") square of olive green wool felt

15cm x 21cm wide (6" x 8¼") piece of thin wadding

15cm (6") embroidery hoop

25cm (10") embroidery hoop

12 x 31cm (12") lengths of 26 gauge white paper-covered wire

29.5cm x 21cm (A4) piece of firm card

29.5cm x 21cm (A4) piece of template plastic

2m x 5mm wide (2yd 8" x ³/₁₆") tight weave cord

Copic markers to match thread colours (optional)

Ruler

Clear craft glue

Fabric adhesive

Tracing paper

Fine black pen

Heat-soluble fabric marker

Sharp HB pencil

NEEDLES

No. 16 chenille

No. 20 chenille

No. 8 crewel

THREADS

Anchor stranded cotton

A = 48 pale blush

B = 66 vy lt wine

C = 69 wine

D = 264 vy lt avocado

DMC no. 5 perlé cotton

E = 3012 med khaki green

F = 3053 green-grey

DMC stranded cotton

G = 310 black

H = 734 lt olive green

I = 816 garnet

J = 915 plum

K = 3011 dk khaki green

L = 3046 med yellow-beige

M = 3053 green-grey

N = 3687 tea rose

O = 3689 lt tea rose

preparation for embroidery

PREPARING THE FABRICS

Cut the piece of quilters muslin into four, 20cm (8") squares.

Cut one 6cm x 21cm wide (2⅜" x 8¼") strip from the firm card and template plastic. With the edges aligned with the straight grain, centre the card strip on the green homespun and trace around the shape with the heat-soluble fabric marker. Cut a 6cm x 21cm wide (2⅜" x 8¼") strip of thin wadding. On the wrong side of the homespun, position the strip of wadding within the marked lines and tack in place. Centre the homespun into the 25cm (10") hoop and tension until taut, taking care to ensure that the lines are not distorted.

TRANSFERRING THE DESIGN

Centre the inner ring of the 15cm (6") hoop on one piece of quilter's muslin. Using the heat-soluble fabric marker,

trace around the inside of the inner ring. Repeat on the remaining three squares. Trace the three petal templates, leaf template and ladybird template onto the tracing paper using the black pen. Using a lightbox or window and working within the marked circles, trace three rosebud centre petals, fifteen small petals, fifteen large petals, one ladybird and eleven leaves evenly distributed between the four pieces of fabric using the heat-soluble fabric marker. Place one of the pieces of fabric with petal shapes into the 15cm (6") hoop and tension until taut.

embroidery

See page 93 for step-by-step instructions for working a rose leaf.

Refer to the close-up photograph for colour placement.

Use the no. 20 chenille needle for the perlé thread, the no. 16 chenille for inserting the wires and the no. 8 crewel needle for all other embroidery.

All embroidery is worked in a hoop.

ORDER OF WORK

OPEN ROSES

There are three open roses and each consists of five large petals and two smaller petals. Each rose is worked in the same manner. Cut a 7.5cm (3") length of wire for each petal.

Large petals

Secure a length of **A** close to the base of one large petal. Leaving a tail at each end, couch the wire around the petal shape. Work two small back stitches inside the shape to secure the thread and bring it to the front just outside the wire at the base of the right-hand side of the petal. Work fifteen close blanket stitches over the wire. Continue working long and short blanket stitch over the wire, bringing the stitches approximately one quarter of the way into the petal and angling each stitch towards the base (diag 1).

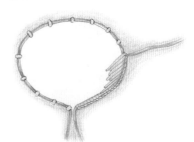

When reaching the equivalent point on the left-hand side of the petal, cover the remaining length of wire at the base with close blanket stitch. Fill the remaining petal area with long and short stitch beginning at the outer edge with **O**, shading through **B** and **N** and finishing at the base with **C**. Work the fifteen large petals in this manner.

Small petals

Stitch the small petals in a similar manner to the large using **O** to couch the wire and work the blanket stitch and long and short blanket stitch. Shade through **B**, **N** and **C** with long and short stitch to complete each petal.

Work six small petals in this manner.

ROSEBUDS

There are three rosebuds and each one consists of one centre petal and three small petals. Cut a 7.5cm (3") length of wire for each petal.

Centre

Using **N**, couch the wire around the petal outline and work the outer edge with blanket stitch and long and short blanket stitch as before, working the stitches two-thirds of the way into the petal. Fill the remaining area with long and short stitch using **C**. Work two centre petals in this manner. Work one centre petal using **C** to couch the wire and work the blanket stitch and long and short blanket stitch, and **J** to work the long and short stitch to fill the remaining area.

Outer petals

Stitch six of the nine remaining small petals in a similar manner to the open rose using **B** for the couching, blanket stitch and long and short blanket stitch, and filling the remaining space with long and short stitch using **N** and **C**. Work the three remaining small petals with **B** for the couching, blanket stitch and long and short blanket stitch and filling the remaining space with long and short stitch using **C** and **J**.

LEAVES

All the leaves are worked in the same manner using three different colourways. Cut a 10cm (4") length of wire for each leaf.

Work five leaves with **K** as the main colour and **M** for the veins, three leaves with **M** as the main colour and **D** for the veins and three leaves with **D** as the main colour and **M** for the veins.

LADYBIRD

Using the ladybird template, cut a small oval of green felt. Stab stitch the felt over the marked shape using two strands of **I**. Using the same thread, work a layer of satin stitch across the shape then a layer of satin stitch down the shape, keeping the edges smooth. Using two strands of **G**, work a straight stitch down the centre of the shape. Using the same thread, at the base of the oval work three straight stitches using the same holes at each end to form the head. Stitch the spots with two small horizontal straight stitches worked over one another using two strands of **G**. Using **D**, work a line of gathering around the ladybird 2mm (¹⁄₁₆") out from the stitching. Carefully apply fabric adhesive around the running stitch, taking care not to touch the stitching. Allow to dry.

Once all petals, leaves and the ladybird are complete, remove the fabric from the hoop and carefully cut out using sharp embroidery scissors. Angle the blades beneath the beaded edge of the blanket stitch on the petals and leaves to obtain a clean, close cut. Cut out the ladybird 2mm (¹⁄₁₆") from the line of running stitch.

If desired, colour the cut edge of the fabric with the *Copic* markers and shape the petals so that the upper edge is curved.

STEMS

Cut thirty-two, 6cm (2³⁄₈") lengths of the cord and apply fabric adhesive to each end of each one to prevent fraying.

Beginning on the left-hand side of the shape, position a piece of cord onto the green homespun in the hoop, aligning the left long edge and upper and lower edges with the lines. Using **F**, hold the cord in place with several small stab stitches around the edge. Using the same thread, cover the cord with satin stitch.

91

Lay a second strip next to the first and stitch in the same manner using **F**. Continue attaching and covering the pieces of cord alternating two strips with **F** and two with **E** until all the lengths of cord are attached. Once all the strips are attached there should be approximately 2cm (¾") uncovered at the right-hand end of the shape.

Remove the fabric from the hoop and cut out the shape leaving a 2.5cm (1") seam allowance. Place on a flat surface, wrong side uppermost. Apply a thin layer of craft glue to one side of the strip of firm card. Press the card strip, glue side down, to the back of the embroidered shape. Allow to dry.

Apply a thin layer of craft glue to the wrong side of the seam allowance on each end of the fabric. Fold in, over the card, and press in place. Repeat on the upper and lower edges. Allow to dry.

CONSTRUCTING THE FLOWER POT

Sides

At the right-hand end of the strip, apply a thin layer of craft glue to the uncovered fabric. Curve the left-hand end of the strip around and press in place over the glued area to form the pot sides.

Hold in place with clips or pegs until the glue is dry.

Lining

Slide the strip of template plastic down inside and adjust so that it sits firmly against the sides. Mark the upper edge of the plastic where it overlaps. Remove and trim so that it fits exactly without any overlap. Centre and glue one strip of green felt to one side of the plastic, trimming the short felt ends only if it is too long. Secure a 70cm (28") length of **E** to the inner top edge of the pot sides. Slide the felt covered plastic strip, felt side innermost, down inside the pot sides. Work blanket stitch, with the stitches 5mm (³⁄₁₆") apart to secure the top edge of the felt to the upper edge of the pot. At the remaining end of the pot overcast the felt to the pot edge with stitches 5mm (³⁄₁₆") apart using **M**.

Base

Using the base template, cut one from the firm card and one from the template plastic to create the base circle. Glue the two circles together and allow to dry. Trace the template onto the olive green felt twice. Cut out one piece of felt 5mm (³⁄₁₆") smaller than the outline and one piece 5mm (³⁄₁₆") larger. Using two strands of **M** and leaving a tail at each end, work a line of gathering around the edge of the larger circle of green felt. Centre the base circle, plastic side down, over the larger circle of felt and pull up the gathering threads firmly and tie off securely. Trim away the excess thread. Apply a thin layer of glue to the exposed card side of the base circle. Position the smaller felt circle over the card and press in place. Centre the pot sides over the base.

Using **E**, stitch the base to the base end of the pot sides with blanket stitch in the same manner as the top edge.

PREPARING THE LID

Trace the lid template onto the olive green felt. Using the heat-soluble marker, mark three, 3cm (1¼") circles on the felt (diag 2).

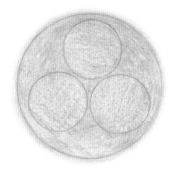

The open roses will be applied within these circles. Begin by applying two small petals opposite one another in the same manner as the hydrangea petals. Apply one large petal to one side then continue adding the remaining four large petals, overlapping each one. Repeat with the remaining two sets of open rose petals. Using two strands of **L** and **H**, work French knots to fill the centre of each rose.

With the right side outermost, curl a centre bud petal around on itself. Position one outer petal on the opposite side to the rolled edge of the centre petal. Add the second and third petals so that the centre is surrounded and carefully twist the wire tails together securely. Repeat for the remaining two sets of bud petals. Working between the open roses, attach the buds to the felt in the same manner as the hydrangea petals.

constructing the lid

See the liftout pattern.

Attaching the leaves

Position the leaves around the outer edge of the upper lid under the rose petals with the tips exposed. Using matching thread, catch the leaf edge to the felt in several places on each side. Continue adding leaves around the outer edge overlapping as necessary.

Finishing

Apply a small dab of craft glue to the underside of the ladybird and glue in place at the desired position. Shape the petals and leaves as desired.

ROSE LEAF

Secure the thread within the leaf base. After the wire is couched, trim any excess wire inside the leaf tip. Use the main thread colour for couching the wire, blanket stitch and satin stitch, changing to the second colour for all veins.

1 | Couch the wire around the leaf, beginning at the base and ending at the tip of the centre vein.

2 | Cover the wire around the outer edge with close blanket stitch.

3 | Cover the centre vein with overcasting using two strands of the vein colour.

4 | Fill one side with angled satin stitch, beginning at the centre and completing one half at a time.

5 | Repeat for the remaining side.

6 | Add four or five straight stitch veins along each side using the vein colour.

jacobean hunt

before you begin

We recommend that you read the complete article

See the liftout pattern for the embroidery design

All embroidery is worked with ONE strand of thread unless specified

this design uses

Brick stitch / Couching
Fly stitch / French knot
Leaf stitch / Long and short stitch
Outline stitch / Padded satin stitch
Seeding / Straight stitch
Trellis couching

The finished design measures 42cm x 48cm wide (16½" x 19").

requirements

FABRIC

56cm x 64cm wide (22" x 25") piece of natural linen twill

SUPPLIES

Light grey sewing thread

Slate frame or stretcher bars to fit fabric

Lacing thread (slate frame)

Thumb tacks (stretcher bars)

Fine black pen

Tracing paper

Fine heat-soluble fabric marker

NEEDLES

No. 2 crewel
No. 10 milliner's

THREADS & BEADS

Appleton's crewel wool
A = 153 vy lt mid blue
B = 154 lt mid blue
C = 155 mid blue
D = 156 med mid blue
E = 157 dk mid blue
F = 158 vy dk mid blue
G = 159 ultra dk mid blue
H = 224 bright terracotta
I = 225 med bright terracotta
J = 227 vy dk bright terracotta
K = 241 vy lt olive green
L = 242 lt olive green
M = 243 olive green

N = 244 med olive green
O = 245 dk olive green
P = 253 med grass green
Q = 291 ultra lt Jacobean green
R = 297 vy dk Jacobean green
S = 311 vy lt brown olive
T = 328 ultra dk dull marine blue
U = 331 vy lt drab green
V = 333 drab green
W = 338 ultra vy dk drab green
X = 473 lt autumn yellow
Y = 504 dk scarlet
Z = 505 vy dk scarlet
AA = 641 ultra lt peacock blue
AB = 643 lt peacock blue
AC = 644 peacock blue
AD = 693 lt honeysuckle yellow
AE = 694 honeysuckle yellow
AF = 695 med honeysuckle yellow
AG = 696 dk honeysuckle yellow
AH = 697 vy dk honeysuckle yellow
AI = 764 med biscuit brown
AJ = 834 med bright peacock green
AK = 904 med golden brown
AL = 905 dk golden brown
AM = 926 dk dull China blue
AN = 947 vy dk bright rose pink
AO = 948 ultra dk bright rose pink

Miyuki no. 15 seed beads
AP = 401 black (4)

preparation for embroidery

PREPARING THE FABRIC

Neaten the edges of the linen with a machine zigzag or overlock stitch to prevent fraying.

TRANSFERRING THE DESIGN

Using the black pen trace the embroidery design, placement marks and numbers onto the tracing paper. Tape the paper to a lightbox or window and centre the linen over the tracing, aligning the placement marks with the straight grain of the fabric. Transfer the design and numbers using the heat-soluble fabric marker. Mount the fabric on the frame ensuring that the surface is taut.

embroidery

See page 103 for step-by-step instructions for working brick stitch.

Refer to the close-up photographs for colour placement.

Use the crewel needle for all embroidery and the milliner's needle for applying the bead eyes.

All embroidery is worked in a frame.

ORDER OF WORK

ACORNS

All acorns are stitched in the same manner using different colours. The kernel on each one is worked in padded satin stitch with two strands of thread. Work layers of straight stitch padding until the kernel is the desired height, finishing with a layer across the shape, then cover with a layer of satin stitch worked down the shape. Work trellis couching over the satin stitch using one strand of thread. Fill the cap with French knots using two strands of thread. Stitch the knots around the outline of the shape first then fill the remaining area. Work a French knot at the tip of the kernel with two strands. The stems are worked in outline stitch after the acorns and leaves have been completed. Using the photograph as a guide, continue each stem into the larger stems as indicated.

Acorn 1

KERNEL: padded satin stitch = **AH**, trellis couching = **O** straight stitch; **M** couching, French knot tip = **R**

CAP: French knot = **R**

STEM: **R**

Acorn 2

KERNEL: padded satin stitch = **AG**, trellis couching = **O** straight stitch; **M** couching, French knot tip = **O**

CAP: French knot = **O**

STEM: **AH**

Acorn 3

KERNEL: padded satin stitch = **G**, trellis couching = **AG** straight stitch; **AH** couching, French knot tip = **G**

CAP: French knot = **O**

STEM: **AH**, **G**

Acorn 4

KERNEL: padded satin stitch = **AG**, trellis couching = **AD** straight stitch; **C** and **V** couching, French knot tip = **O**

CAP: French knot = **O**

Acorn 5

KERNEL: padded satin stitch = **AE**, trellis couching = **K** straight stitch; **C** and **AG** couching, French knot tip = **N**

CAP: French knot = **N**

STEM: **N**, **AE**

Acorn 6

KERNEL: padded satin stitch = **F**, trellis couching = **AL** straight stitch; **AK** couching, French knot tip = **AJ**

CAP: French knot = **AJ**

STEM: **AJ**

Acorn 7

KERNEL: padded satin stitch = **M**, trellis couching = **AG** straight stitch; **AE** couching, French knot tip = **AC**

CAP: French knot = **AC**

STEM: **M**, **AG**

Acorn 8

KERNEL: padded satin stitch = **AL**, trellis couching = **F** straight stitch; **AG** couching, French knot tip = **V**

CAP: French knot = **V**

STEM: **AK**

Acorn 9

KERNEL: padded satin stitch = **R**, trellis couching = **L** straight stitch; **U** and **AH** couching, French knot tip = **AD**

CAP: French knot = **AD**

STEM: **E**, **AF**, **AJ**

Acorn 10

KERNEL: padded satin stitch = **AF**, trellis couching = **AG** straight stitch; **F** and **O** couching, French knot tip = **O**

CAP: French knot = **O**

STEM: **O**

Acorn 11

KERNEL: padded satin stitch = **AH**, trellis couching = **O** straight stitch; **F** couching, French knot tip = **F**

CAP: French knot = **F**

STEM: **F**

Acorn 12

KERNEL: padded satin stitch = **AH**, trellis couching = **F** straight stitch; **M** couching, French knot tip = **O**

CAP: French knot = **O**

STEM: **O**

Acorn 13

KERNEL: padded satin stitch = **R**, trellis couching = **N** straight stitch; **U** couching, French knot tip = **AF**

CAP: French knot = **AF**

STEM: **E**, **R**, **AH**

OAK LEAVES

All leaves are worked in long and short stitch. The outer colour is worked first with two strands of thread and the remaining colours are worked with one strand. Angle the stitches towards the leaf tips. The colours are listed in the order that they are worked from the outer edge to the centre vein. The centre vein is worked last in outline stitch using one or two colours and continues to create the stem. Use the photograph as a guide to colour and stitch placement.

Leaf 1: **F**, **R**; vein: **L**, **AG**

Leaf 2: **V**, **R**; vein: **R**, **AG**

Leaf 3: **E**, **G**; vein: **R**, **AG**

Leaf 4: **M**, **V**; vein: **C**, **O**

Leaf 5: **AG**, **AH**, **AL**; vein: **AL**

Leaf 6: **T**, **O**, **M**, **AG**; vein: **O**, **AH**

Leaf 7: **L**, **AD**; vein: **E**, **AG**

Leaf 8: **V**, **AB**; vein: **AC**, **AG**

Leaf 9: **O**, **AL**; vein: **AG**, **AL**

Leaf 10: **M**, **O**; vein: **O**, **AH**

Leaf 11: **O**, **L**, **V**; vein: **L**

Leaf 12: **K**, **L**; vein: **O**, **AE**

Leaf 13: **N**, **AM**; vein: **F**, **R**

Leaf 14: **V**, **L**; vein: **O**

Leaf 15: **W**, **N**; vein: **F**

Leaf 16: **AD**, **K**, **L**, **M**; vein: **M**, **AG**

Using **T** work a closed fly stitch leaf below leaf 15.

GRAPES

All grapes are stitched in the same manner using different colours. Each one is worked in padded satin stitch with two strands of thread. Work layers of straight stitch padding until the grape is the desired height, finishing with a layer across the shape, then cover with a layer of satin stitch worked down the shape. The shape is then covered with rows of straight stitch couched in place with three or four stitches and surrounded with a row of outline stitch using one strand. The stems are worked in stem stitch using one strand and should be completed only after the leaves and leaf stems have been worked.

Grape 1: padded satin stitch = **I**, couched straight stitch and outline = **AN**; stem = **F**

Grape 2: padded satin stitch = **J**, couched straight stitch and outline = **AN**; stem = **F**

Grape 3: padded satin stitch = **AO**, couched straight stitch and outline = **AN**; stem = **AI**

Grape 4: padded satin stitch = **J**, couched straight stitch and outline = **AN**; stem = **AI**

Grape 5: padded satin stitch = **AO**, couched straight stitch and outline = **AN**; stem = **F**

Grape 6: padded satin stitch = **I**, couched straight stitch and outline = **AN**; stem = **F**

Grape 7: padded satin stitch = **I**, couched straight stitch and outline = **AN**; stem = **AC**

Grape 8: padded satin stitch = **I**, couched straight stitch and outline = **AN**; stem = **F**

Grape 9: padded satin stitch = **J**, couched straight stitch and outline = **AN**; stem = **F**

Grape 10: padded satin stitch = **AO**, couched straight stitch and outline = **AN**; stem = **AI**

Grape 11: padded satin stitch = **Z**, couched straight stitch and outline = **AN**

Grape 12: padded satin stitch = **Z**, couched straight stitch and outline = **AN**; stem = **AI**

GRAPE LEAVES

All leaves are worked in long and short stitch. The outer colour is worked first with two strands of thread and the remaining colours are worked with one strand. Angle the stitches towards the leaf tips. The colours are listed in the order that they are worked from the outer edge to the centre vein. The veins are worked last in outline stitch using one strand and some continue to create the stem. Use the photograph as a guide to colour and stitch placement.

Leaf 1: **T**, **AM**, **O**; vein = **M**

Leaf 2: **D**, **G**; vein = **O**

Leaf 3: **G**, **AM**; vein = **AB**

Leaf 4: **AB**, **F**; vein = **G**

Leaf 5: **T**, **AC**; vein = **L**

Leaf 6: **AJ**, **AM**, **G**; vein = **AE**

Leaf 7: **G**, **AM**; vein = **O**

Leaf 8: **AM**, **G**; vein = **D**

Work a closed fly stitch leaf just below leaf 7 using two strands of **AC** and **D**. Add an outline stitch stem with two strands of **AC**, working along the lower edge of the main stem. Stitch a pair of closed fly stitch leaves above leaf 8 using two strands of **T** for the upper leaf and two strands of **F** for the lower leaf. Add a small outline stitch stem to the upper leaf using two strands of **F**.

TREE TRUNK

The trunk is worked in brick stitch using two strands of **L**, **K** and **S**. Begin on one side and work across the shape. Use the photograph as a guide to colour placement. Work a closed fly stitch leaf below the bird's tail using **F**. Add a stem in outline stitch using the same thread.

HILLOCKS

Each hillock is worked in long and short stitch with the outer colour worked first using two strands of thread and the remaining colours worked with a single strand.

Hillock 1: **AD**, **L**, **AB** and **F**

Hillock 2: **AF**, **M** and **D**

Hillock 3: **F** and **T**

Hillock 4: **AD**, **L**, **AB** and **AM**

Hillock 5: **AD**, **L**, **O** and **T**

Hillock 6: **S**, **L** and **AB**

Hillock 7: **A**, **B** and **AM**

RED FLOWER

Petals

Each flower petal is worked in long and short stitch with the outer colour worked first using two strands of thread and the remaining colours worked with a single strand. Stitch the five central petals beginning with **Y** on the outer edge and shading through **Z** to **J** at the centre. Work the outer petals beginning with **H** on the outer edges shading to **AN**.

Sepals

Stitch the sepals with closed fly stitch using **O** and **F** for the left-hand se~~p~~all and **O** for the right-hand se~~p~~.

Stem

Work the stem ~~i~~ ~~c~~ose rows of outline stitch begi~~nn~~ng on the left-hand side with ~~c~~hanging to two strands of **K**, **L**, ~~L~~, **N** and **F**.

Leaves

All leaves are stitched with two strands of thread. Stitch the two upper leaves on the stem in closed fly stitch using **N** and **W** for the left-hand leaf and **N** and **O** for the right-hand leaf. Stitch the stem lower leaf in satin stitch using **AH**. Work the two leaves just above the petals in leaf stitch using **F** and **AM** for the left-hand leaf and **F** for the right-hand leaf. Stitch the stem in outline stitch using **F**.

YELLOW FLOWER

Petals

Each flower petal is worked in long and short stitch with the outer colour worked first using two strands of

thread and the remaining colour worked with a single strand. Stitch the five petals beginning with **U** on the outer edge and changing to **AD** at the centre. Work the centre vein in outline stitch using **AE**.

Sepals

Work the sepals in the same manner as the petals beginning with **U** on the outer edge and changing to **K** at the centre. Stitch the centre vein in outline stitch using **K**.

Centre

Outline the centre with outline stitch using **AE**. Fill the outer area with trellis couching using **V** for the straight stitches. Couch each intersection with a

cross using **B** and a straight stitch using **AH**. Fill the centre shape with French knots using two strands of **AF**.

Stem

Work the stem in outline stitch beginning on the left-hand side with **K** changing to two strands of **L** then **N**. Work a second line of **N** with one strand then lines of **AH**, **K** and **AF**.

Leaves

Work all leaves in closed fly stitch using **N** and **O** for the upper left-hand leaf, **O** for the upper right-hand leaf, **L** and **N** for the lower left-hand leaf and **N** and **O** for the lower right-hand leaf.

SMALL DEER

The body and legs of the deer are worked in long and short stitch and the head, back legs and tail are worked in satin stitch. Work the head and ears with **AK**. Using two strands of **AK** stitch the upper back and outer chest, changing to **AH** to complete the body. Work the front legs using **AI**, **AK** and **AH** and the back legs with **AH** and **AI**. Stitch the tail with **AK**. Stitch a bead

(**AP**) in place for the eye using the light grey sewing thread.

STAG

The body of the stag is worked in long and short stitch and the head, legs and tail are worked in satin stitch.

Work the head and ears using two strands of **AL**. Work the right-hand edge of the neck and back with the same thread. Stitch the left-hand edge of the neck with two strands of **AH**. Fill the remainder of the body with **AH**, **AI**, **AK** and **AL** using the photograph as a guide to colour placement. Work the straight front leg with **AL** and the bent leg with **AG**. Stitch the tail and right-hand back leg with **AK** and the left-hand back leg with **AH**. Using two strands of **AG**, work the antlers with French knots. Stitch a bead (**AP**) in place for the eye using the light grey sewing thread.

DOG

The head, body and back legs of the dog are worked in long and short stitch and the ear and front legs are worked in satin stitch. Using two strands of **AI**, stitch the muzzle, upper head, upper neck and back. Work the bottom jaw, lower head and remaining body area with **AH**. Complete the front and back legs using **AH** and **AI**. Stitch the ear with two strands of **AH** and the tail with two strands of **AI**. Attach a bead (**AP**) for the eye using the light grey sewing thread.

SMALL LEAFY TREES

All leaves are worked with two strands of thread and the stems are worked with one strand. Stitch the left-hand tree leaves with closed fly stitch using **G** for the four upper leaves, **F** for the fifth leaf and **AM** for the remaining leaves. Work the stems in outline stitch using **G** for the upper section, **F** for the fifth leaf and **AM** for the lower stem.

Work the centre tree leaves with satin stitch using **L** and **M** for the tip and right-hand tip leaves, **L** for the left-hand tip leaf, **M** for the centre leaf, **O** for the lower left-hand leaf and **M** for the lower

right-hand leaf. Add an outline stitch vein on the tip and left-hand tip leaves using **L** and work the upper stem in outline stitch with the same thread. Add a vein in the same manner to the centre and lower right-hand leaves using **M**. Continue the line of outline stitch from the lower right-hand leaf down to the hillock to form the stem.

Stitch the right-hand tree leaves in closed fly stitch using **AJ** for the tip leaf, **F** for the right-hand tip and **D** for the left-hand tip leaves. Work the left-hand centre leaf with **D** and **F** and the right-hand centre and lower leaves with **F**. Stitch a single closed fly stitch leaf between the small deer legs using two strands of **F**.

SOLID TREES

Each tree is worked in long and short stitch using two strands for the upper colour and one strand for any remaining colours. Working from left to right begin the first tree with **AJ** at the tip and shade through **F** to **G** at the base. Work the next tree with **AM**, the next tree with **N** at the outer edge and **AM** at the base, the next tree with **AM** at the outer edge and **F** at the base and the last tree with **AB** at the outer edge and **F** at the base.

STRAWBERRIES

The strawberries are worked with padded satin stitch with seed stitch details. The sepals are worked in straight stitch and the stem with outline stitch.

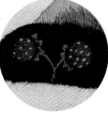

Fill the berries on hillock 3 with layers of straight stitch padding then cover with satin stitch using **Y**. Work the seeds with **AF** and the sepals and stem with **AB**.

Fill the berries on hillock 5 with layers of straight stitch padding then cover with satin stitch using **AN**. Work the seeds with **AE** and the sepals and stem with **AB**.

BIRD

Beak

Work the beak in satin stitch using **AG**.

Feet

Stitch the feet with rows of outline stitch using **AG**.

Head and body

The head and body are worked in long and short stitch.

Using two strands of **P** work the top of the head. Stitch the throat and upper chest with two strands of **C**. Fill the remaining head and body with **A**, **B**, **AA** and **AB** using the photograph as a guide to colour placement. Using **AG** work outline stitch around the eye. Stitch a bead (**AP**) in the centre of the eye with the light grey sewing thread. Work a row of outline stitch around the bead using **AE**.

Wings

Stitch the right-hand edge of the upper wing with long and short stitch using two strands of **AC** for the outer row and **Y** for the inner row. Work the upper edge of the lower wing in the same manner using two strands of **AC** for the outer row and **AN** for the inner row.

Embroider the feathers in close leaf stitch alternating **A**, **AM** and **AE**.

Tail

Work the tail feathers in the same manner as the wing feathers with **AA**, **C** and **AE** and using the photograph as a guide to colour placement.

FINISHING

Remove any visible design lines with a hair dryer. Remove the fabric from the frame and make up as required.

BRICK STITCH

Offset blocks of satin stitch form the striking filling used for the main stem. Mark in guidelines to help keep the stitches even.

To help maintain stitch direction along a shape, begin at the centre of one edge and complete one side of the first row at a time. Continue across the area in the same manner.

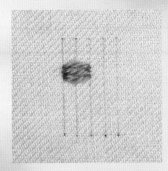

1 | First row. Work a small block of long stitches from the edge to the second guideline.

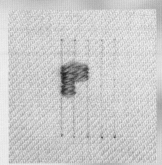

2 | Work a block of short stitches from the edge to the first guideline.

3 | Complete the row, alternating blocks of long and short stitches.

4 | Second row. Change colour. Work blocks of long stitches from the first short blocks to the third guideline.

5 | Third row. Work blocks of long stitches between those of the previous row.

6 | Continue working rows in the same manner, changing colour as required

7 | Final row. At the edge of the shape work alternating blocks of long and short stitches.

red currants

before you begin

We recommend that you read the complete article

See the liftout pattern for the templates

All embroidery is worked with ONE strand of thread unless specified

this design uses

Blanket stitch / Fly stitch
Long and short stitch
Stem stitch / Straight stitch
Wrapping

The finished spray measures 12cm x 21cm wide (4¾" x 8¼").

requirements

FABRIC
30cm (12") square of green cotton homespun

SUPPLIES
Green sewing thread
26 gauge beading wire
10mm (³⁄₈") red wooden beads (20)
18.5cm (7¼") dry wooden stem with four junctions
20cm (8") embroidery hoop
Glue (clear and fast drying)
Fine paintbrush
Long-nose pliers
Drill and 1.5mm, 2.5mm and 3.5mm drill bits
3mm drill bit (optional)
Tracing paper
Fine black pen
Fine heat-soluble fabric marker
Fine air-soluble fabric marker
Aerosol gloss sealer

NEEDLE
No. 3 crewel

THREADS
Gumnut Yarns Daisies fine wool
A = 604 lt rainforest
B = 607 med rainforest
C = 608 dk rainforest
D = 829 dk peach Melba
E = 969 dk chocolate dip

preparation for embroidery

TRANSFERRING THE DESIGN

Using the inner ring of the embroidery hoop, trace a circle onto the tracing paper. Taking care to ensure that the base of each leaf is facing the circle outline, trace the five leaf templates and leaf numbers onto the tracing paper, omitting the veins. Tape the tracing to a lightbox or window. Centre the square of green homespun over the tracing and transfer the leaf shaping to the fabric with the heat-soluble pen. Make a note of the leaf number just outside the outline of each one. Place the fabric in the hoop tensioning it until the surface is taut.

embroidery

Refer to the close-up photograph for colour placement.

All embroidery is worked in the hoop.

ORDER OF WORK

LEAVES

Leaf 1

Leaving a 6cm (2⅜") tail at each end and using the green sewing thread, couch the beading wire around the outline of the leaf. Beginning at the base, work close blanket stitch over the wire using **B**. Using the same thread, fill the leaf with long and short stitch, fanning the stitches from the base up into the leaf tips. Mark the primary veins onto the leaf surface with the air-soluble marker. Beginning at the base and using **A**, stitch the veins with stem stitch. Mark in and stitch the small, secondary veins with fly stitch and straight stitch using the same thread.

A is also used to wrap the leaf stem. If you have enough thread remaining to do this, bring it to the base of the leaf through the stitches on the back. Secure it to the wire, just below the leaf, with a small amount of glue. Allow to dry.

Leaf 2

Work the leaf in the same manner as leaf 1 leaving 3cm (1⅛") wire tails.

Leaf 3

Work the leaf in the same manner as leaf 1 leaving 9cm (3½") wire tails.

Leaf 4

Work the leaf in the same manner as leaf 1 leaving 9cm (3½") wire tails and using **C** for the blanket stitch and long and short stitch and **B** for the veins. **B** is also used to wrap the leaf stem.

Leaf 5

Work the leaf in the same manner as leaf 4 leaving 7.5cm (3") wire tails.

WRAPPING THE STEMS

Carefully cut out each leaf taking care not to cut any remaining threads. If the remaining vein thread is insufficient in length to wrap the stem, glue a new thread in place. With a 1cm (⅜") tail facing away from the leaf, glue the thread to the wire just below the leaf (diag 1).

Allow to dry.

Wrap the stem of each leaf to the end of the wire and anchor with glue. Allow to dry. Trim the remaining wrapping thread on leaves 1, 2, 3 and 4. Do not cut the excess thread on leaf 5.

RED CURRANTS

Note: The hole at the centre of each bead needs to be at least 3mm (⅛") in diameter. If it is smaller use the drill with the 3mm drill bit to enlarge it.

Cut a 1.2m (1yd 11") length of **D**. Leaving a 5cm (2") tail, wrap the bead covering the surface completely. Anchor the thread tails by catching them through the threads lining the centre. Trim away the remainder of the 5cm (2") tail and leave the second tail at one end of the bead (diag 2).

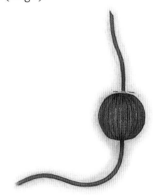

This will be the base of the red currant. Repeat with the remaining beads.

STEM

Note: The depth of the stem at each junction should not be less than 1.5cm (⅝"). This allows 1cm (⅜") of the covered wire to be inserted into the stem without drilling through it completely, giving a neater and more natural appearance.

Wash the piece of dry stem removing any loose bark and dirt. Allow to dry. Seal the entire surface with several coats of aerosol gloss sealer in a well-ventilated area, allowing the sealer to dry between coats.

The placement of the holes will depend entirely on the shape of the stem being used.

On Julie's stem, three leaves are attached close to the base, three racemes of redcurrants are attached further along the stem, then a single, small leaf and lastly, a small single raceme of three red currants and a single small leaf are attached at the tip.

Using the drill and the 3.5mm bit, drill a 1cm (⅜") deep hole at the point where the triple stem of red currants will be attached. Using the 2.5mm bit, drill a 1cm (⅜") deep hole at the points where the three leaves are attached near the

stem base and the single stem of red currants and single leaf are attached near the stem tip. Use the 1.5mm bit to drill a 1cm (³⁄₈") hole at the point that the single small leaf will be attached.

> **HINT:** If you have a length of stem that does not have obvious junctions, drill 1cm (³⁄₈") holes, at an angle, into the stem at the positions indicated but do not go right through it.

RED CURRANT RACEMES

> **NOTE:** Each red currant has a stalk that is attached to a stem, making up the raceme. The stalks are created by inserting a length of beading wire with a hooked end down through the bead hole so that the hook catches on the threads lining the hole.

Cut the following lengths of beading wire:
Raceme 1: 8 x 12.5cm (5")
Raceme 2: 6 x 9.5cm (3³⁄₄")
Raceme 3: 3 x 4cm (1¹⁄₂")
Raceme 4: 3 x 3.5cm (1³⁄₈")

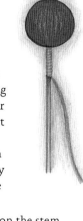

At one end of each length of wire bend a 5mm (³⁄₁₆") hook with the long-nose pliers. Push the end of the hook slightly towards the wire length (diag 3).

Insert the straight end of each wire from the top down through the centre of one bead and pull through until the hook catches the threads lining the centre (diag 4).

Repeat with the remaining beads and hooked wires.

Raceme 1

Raceme 1 has eight red currants along the stem and uses the beads with the 12.5cm (5") stems. Before assembling the raceme, the brown tufts are added at the tip of each red currant and the stalks are wrapped.

Cut two, 2cm (³⁄₄") lengths of **E**. Cut a 140cm (1yd 19") length of **A**. This thread will be used to wrap the stalk of the end bead and attach the seven remaining currant stalks to the stem. Thread the length of **A** into the crewel needle. Leaving a 1.5cm (⁵⁄₈") tail, take the needle up through the base of a bead and emerge at the top. Lay the two lengths of **E** across the centre hole at the top and take the needle back down through the centre hole (diag 5).

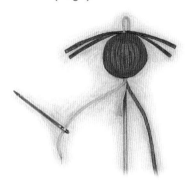

Holding the tail at the base, pull the thread firmly so that the short lengths are pulled down into the hole, leaving the ends emerging at the top (diag 6).

Anchor the tail of **D**, the 1.5cm (⁵⁄₈") tail and the long thread of **A** to the wire as close to the bead as possible with a small amount of glue. Allow the glue to dry. Using the long thread, wrap the wire and thread tails for 1.5cm (⁵⁄₈"). Anchor the wrapping thread with glue and allow to dry. Trim the short thread tails if required but do not cut the long wrapping thread.

To work the tufts and stalks of the seven remaining beads cut fourteen, 2cm (³⁄₄") lengths of **E** and seven, 10cm (4") lengths of **A**. Repeat the previous procedure with four beads, wrapping the wire stem and tails for 1cm (³⁄₈"). Repeat the procedure with the three remaining beads wrapping the wire stem and tails for 5mm (³⁄₁₆"). Trim the short thread tails at the end of the wrapping on all seven stalks but do not cut away the remaining wire or the wrapping thread (diag 7).

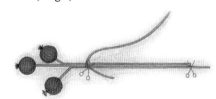

Beginning with the bead on the stem that is wrapped for 1.5cm (⁵⁄₈") as the tip of the raceme, attach the seven bead stalks with the long thread of **A**, aligning the ends of the wrapping and beginning at the tip end. Alternate the beads from side to side and incorporate each wire and thread tail into the stem as the bead stalks are wrapped in place. Use the diagram below as a guide (diag 8).

As each currant stalk is attached, anchor the wrapping thread with glue and allow to dry. Wrap each wire and thread tail to the stem until reaching the point that the next stalk is applied. Trim away the thread tail but do not cut the long wrapping thread. Trim the wire so that it is the same length as the raceme tip bead wire (diag 9).

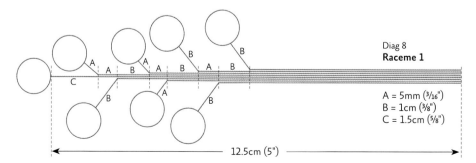

Diag 8
Raceme 1

A = 5mm (³⁄₁₆")
B = 1cm (³⁄₈")
C = 1.5cm (⁵⁄₈")

12.5cm (5")

After applying the last stalk wrap the stem, thread tail and stalk wire for 1cm (⅜") then trim away the excess thread tail. Trim the wire to the same length as the raceme tip bead wire as before. You should have eight wires in the stem bundle that are all the same length. Continue wrapping the wires to the end. Anchor the thread with glue and allow to dry. Leave the remaining thread. Trim the tuft at the tip of each red currant to 3mm (⅛") and fluff out the fibres.

Raceme 2

Raceme 2 has six red currants along the stem and uses the beads with the 9.5cm (3¾") stems. Before assembling the raceme, the brown tufts are added at the tip of each red currant and the stalks are wrapped.

Cut twelve, 2cm (¾") lengths of **E**. Cut five 10cm (4") lengths and a 120cm (1yd 11") length of **A**.

Each red currant other than the tip has a 1cm (⅜") wrapped stalk.

Add the tufts, wrap the stalks and assemble the raceme in the same manner as raceme 1 using the diagram below as a guide to placement (diag 10).

Raceme 3

Raceme 3 has three red currants along the stem and uses the beads with the 4cm (1½") stems. Before assembling the raceme, the brown tufts are added at the tip of each red currant and the stalks are wrapped. Cut six, 2cm (¾") lengths of **E**. Cut two, 10cm (4") lengths and a 20cm (8") length of **A**.

Each red currant other than the tip has a 5mm (³⁄₁₆") wrapped stalk.

Add the tufts, wrap the stalks and assemble the raceme in the same manner

as raceme 1 using the diagram as a guide to placement (diag 11).

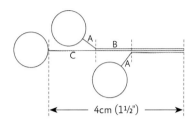

← 4cm (1½") →

Raceme 4

Raceme 4 has three red currants along the stem and uses the beads with the 3.5cm (1⅜") stems. Before assembling the raceme, the brown tufts are added at the tip of each red currant and the stalks are wrapped. Cut six, 2cm (¾") lengths of **E**. Cut two, 10cm (4") lengths and a 20cm (8") length of **A**.

Each red currant other than the tip has a 1cm (⅜") wrapped stalk.

Add the tufts, wrap the stalks and assemble the raceme in the same manner as raceme 1 using the diagram as a guide to placement (diag 12).

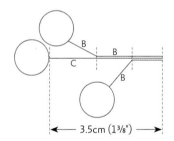

← 3.5cm (1⅜") →

Assembling the red currant stems and leaves

Some of the stems and leaves are attached to one another to make insertion into the wooden stem easier.

Align the stem ends of racemes 1, 2 and 3 and anchor with glue. Trim away the

excess wrapping thread on stems 2 and 3 only. Using the excess thread from stem 1 wrap 5mm (³⁄₁₆") at the base around all stems (diag 13).

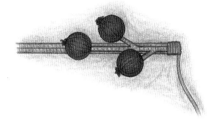

Thread the remaining length into the crewel needle and run it back under the wraps to secure. Trim the excess thread.

Attach the ends of raceme 4 and leaf 2 in the same manner, using the excess wrapping thread from the raceme.

Assemble leaves 3, 4 and 5 in the same manner using the excess wrapping thread on leaf 5.

Attaching the red currants and leaves to the wooden stem

Using the photograph as a guide to positioning and working quickly, brush glue into the 3.5mm hole using the paint brush. Take care to ensure that the glue is applied right into the base of the hole. Brush glue onto the wrapped end of the attached group of three red currant racemes and push firmly into the hole. Attach the group of three leaves into the 2.5mm hole near the base of the wooden stem, the attached red currant raceme and leaf into the 2.5mm hole at the stem tip and the single leaf into the 1.5mm hole in the same manner. Allow to dry.

Finishing

Arrange the leaves and racemes in a pleasing manner using the photograph as a guide.

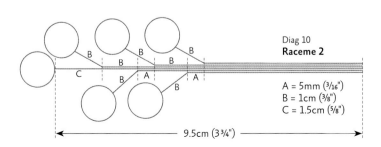

Diag 10
Raceme 2

A = 5mm (³⁄₁₆")
B = 1cm (⅜")
C = 1.5cm (⅝")

← 9.5cm (3¾") →

le magnolia

before you begin

We recommend that you read the complete article

See the liftout pattern for the embroidery design and stitch direction diagram

All embroidery is worked with ONE strand of thread

this design uses

Long and short stitch
Satin stitch / Stem stitch
Straight stitch

The finished design measures 14cm x 17cm wide (5½" x 6¾").

requirements

FABRIC

25cm x 35cm wide (10" x 14") piece of fine white linen

SUPPLIES

Slate frame or stretcher bars to fit fabric
Lacing thread (slate frame)
Thumb tacks (stretcher bars)
Fine black pen
Tracing paper
Fine heat-soluble fabric marker

NEEDLE

No. 10 crewel

THREADS

DMC stranded cotton
A = 154 vy dk grape
B = 208 dk lavender
C = 445 lt lemon
D = 469 avocado green
E = 471 vy lt avocado green
F = 472 ultra lt avocado green
G = 601 dk cranberry
H = 640 vy dk beige-grey
I = 718 med fuchsia
J = 772 vy lt yellow-green
K = 777 vy dk raspberry
L = 819 lt baby pink
M = 915 plum
N = 917 dk fuchsia
O = 926 med grey-green
P = 927 lt grey-green
Q = 928 vy lt grey-green
R = 934 black avocado green
S = 936 dk avocado green
T = 937 med avocado green
U = 3021 vy dk Jacobean green
V = 3607 fuchsia
W = 3608 lt fuchsia
X = 3609 vy lt fuchsia
Y = 3756 vy lt baby blue
Z = 3768 dk grey-green
AA = 3787 dk Jacobean green

preparation for embroidery

PREPARING THE FABRIC

Neaten the raw edges of the linen with a machine zigzag or overlock stitch to prevent fraying.

TRANSFERRING THE DESIGN

Using the black pen trace the embroidery design and placement marks onto the tracing paper. Aligning the placement marks with the straight grain, centre the linen over the design and, using a lightbox or window if necessary, transfer the design with the heat-soluble fabric marker.

Attach the fabric to the frame or stretcher bars ensuring that the surface is drum tight.

embroidery

Refer to the close-up photograph for colour placement.

All embroidery is worked in a frame.

ORDER OF WORK

All embroidery is worked with long and short stitch unless specified.

FLOWER ONE

Tepal one

Stitch the centre vein with **A** tapering to a single stitch close to the tip. Stitch the outer edge of the tepal using **A**, **M**, **N** and **V** (fig 1).

Fill the light area near the tepal tip with **X** and add straight stitches on the left-hand side using **J** (fig 2).

Shade the tepal through **W**, **V**, **N**, **M** into **A** at the base. Work straight stitch highlights as indicated using **X** (fig 3).

Tepal two

Stitch the lower section of the centre vein using **D** and the upper section using **D** and **F** (fig 4).

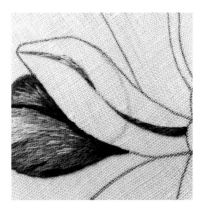

Fill the light, upper section of the tepal with **X** adding straight stitch highlights

with **F** and **Y**. Work the right-hand edge beginning with **V** at the tepal tip and shading into **N** and **B**. Add a few straight stitches in the upper vein using **N** and on the right-hand side of the tepal with **V**. Begin filling the lower section of the tepal with **V** (fig 5).

Fill the remainder of the lower section using **M**, **N** and **V**.

Tepal three

Stitch the vein using **D** and **A**, working stem stitch where necessary. Fill the upper section of the tepal with **L** and **X** then work straight stitches over the area with **C**. Work a few straight stitches at the tip of the tepal using **W** (fig 6).

Fill the remainder of the tepal using **B**, **M**, **N** and **V**, and add highlights with **X**.

Tepal four

Stitch the vein using **D** and **F**. Fill the light upper section using **L**, **W** and **X**, adding straight stitches over the area with **F**. Stitch the lower section using **B** and **V** shading into **M**, **N** and **A** in the darkest areas at the tepal base. Work straight stitches over the upper area of the darker section with **X** to blend the colours.

Tepal five

Before beginning the tepal work the small, green tepals at the base of tepal three using **D** and **F** and at the base of tepal two using **D**, **F** and **R**. Stitch the section of the tepal above tepal four and begin working the lower section using **K**, **N** and **V** (fig 7).

Fill the remainder of the tepal using the same threads.

FLOWER TWO

Tepal one

Stitch the tepal beginning with **A** on the outer edge and shading through **M**, **N** to **V** and finishing with **A** at the base (fig 8).

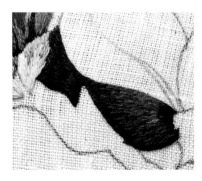

Tepal two

Work the vein with **S** in the lower section and **D** in the upper section. Fill the lower half of the tepal using **B**, **I**, **N** and **X** and the large upper section using **B**, **I**, **K**, **L**, **N** and **X**. Highlight the vein using **A**. Stitch the tip turnover using **C**, **I**, **L** and **W**. Work the vein on the turnover using **A** and highlight the edge of the upper section using **K**.

Tepal three

Stitch the small visible area of tepal three using **A** and **M**.

Tepal four

Stitch the vein using **D** and **F**. Fill the tepal using **B**, **I**, **L**, **M**, **V**, **W** and **X**.

Tepal five

Work the vein using **A**. Fill the tepal beginning with **B** and **V** at the outer edge and shading through **G** to **A** and **M** at the base.

Tepal six

Stitch the vein using **D** and **S**. Fill the large section using **A**, **B**, **L**, **I**, **W** and **X**, adding straight stitches over the light areas using **C**. Stitch the vein on the turnover using **A**. Fill the remainder of the turnover with **M**, shading through **G**, **V** to **C** at the tip.

Tepal seven

Stitch the tepal beginning with **G** and **B**, where indicated, on the outer edge tapering through **M** to **A** at the base.

Small green tepals

Complete the tepals at the base of each flower using **T**, **E**, **F** and **AA**.

STEMS AND BUDS

Stems

Using the photograph as a guide stitch the stems using **F**, **H**, **T**, **U** and **AA**. Work small, scattered straight stitches over the lighter areas using **F** and several longer straight stitches in the stem close to the left-hand leaves using **A**.

Buds

Stitch the small buds using **F** and **T** (fig 9).

Work the large bud at the base of the design with **F**, **T**, **X** and **AA**.

LEAVES

Leaf one

Stitch the left-hand side using **F**, **O**, **P**, **Q**, **T**, **Z** and **AA** (fig 10).

Work the right-hand side of the leaf using **F**, **O**, **P** and **Q** (fig 11).

Work a line of stem stitch along the vein using **Y**. Work a second, partial line of stem stitch using **A**, beginning at the base of the leaf stem and finishing close to the leaf tip. Fill the remaining leaf stem with **AA** and **Z**.

Leaf two

Stitch the left-hand side of the leaf using **L**, **O**, **P**, **Q**, **Z** and **AA**. Work the right-hand side using **F**, **O**, **P**, **Q**, **Y**, **Z** and **AA**. Embroider the stem with stem stitch using **A** extending into the leaf stem. Fill the remaining stem with **AA**.

Leaf three

Work the upper half of the leaf using **D**, **E**, **F**, **R**, **S** and **T**. Stitch the lower half using **B**, **E**, **F**, **S**, **T** and **AA**. Beginning on the outer edge with **O**, work the leaf turnover, shading through **P** to **Q** on the

inner edge. Embroider the vein in stem stitch using **A** (fig 12).

FINISHING

Remove the embroidery from the frame. If necessary remove any visible design lines with a hair dryer. Soak the embroidery in warm soapy water but do not rub the surface. Rinse in clean warm water. Roll in a clean towel to remove most of the moisture then lay on a flat surface away from direct sunlight until almost dry. Place the embroidery, face down, onto a smooth padded surface and press until dry.

versailles chatelaine

before you begin

We recommend that you read the complete article and instructions in the liftout pattern

See the liftout pattern for the embroidery designs and cutting layouts

All embroidery is worked with ONE strand of thread unless specified

this design uses

Back stitch / Blanket stitch
Bullion loop / Bullion knot
Chain stitch / Corded coral stitch
Detached chain / Fly stitch
French knot
Interlaced chain stitch
Running stitch / Satin stitch
Split stitch / Straight stitch
Trellis couching / Twisted cord
Up and down blanket stitch

The *scissor sheath* measures 14cm x 8cm wide (5 1/2" x 3 1/8"), the *scissor fob* meaures 4.7cm x 2.5cm wide (1 7/8" x 1"), the *pinwheel* measures 8cm (3 1/8") in diameter and the *needlebook* measures 10.5cm x 9cm wide (4 1/8" x 3 1/2").

requirements

FABRIC

25cm x 140cm wide (10" x 55") piece of latté silk duchess satin

10cm x 40cm wide (4" x 16") piece of cream wool flannel

SUPPLIES

10cm (4") embroidery hoop
12.5cm (5") embroidery hoop
15cm (6") embroidery hoop
3.5cm (1 3/8") diameter mother-of-pearl rings (3)
3cm (1 3/16") mother-of-pearl heart buckle (1)
White glass head pins (55)
Clear glass pebble bead (1)
25cm x 15mm wide (10" x 5/8") cream and lt blue silk ribbon with ruffled edge
Ivory silk sewing thread
Two, 29.5cm x 21cm wide (A4) pieces of thin, firm card
30cm x 60cm wide (12" x 24") piece of thin fusible wadding
Strong lacing thread
Pinking shears
Craft glue

Fine black pen
Tracing paper
Fine heat-soluble fabric marker

NEEDLES

No. 8 crewel
No. 10 crewel
No. 10 sharp
No. 26 tapestry

THREADS

Au ver a soie, soie d'Alger
stranded silk
A = 1741 vy lt Indian blue
B = 2133 hunter green
C = 2514 buttercup
D = 2931 vy lt carnation
E = 3023 burgundy
F = 3322 vy lt violet
G = 524 golden olive (2)
H = 4100 ivory (2)
I = 4147 ultra lt China rose

DMC no. 5 perlé cotton
J = 832 golden olive

preparation for embroidery

PREPARING THE FABRICS

Cut three 20cm (8") squares and one 15cm (6") square of silk. Neaten the raw edges with a machine zigzag or overlock stitch to prevent fraying.

TRANSFERRING THE DESIGN

> **NOTE:** The embroidery is worked onto the wrong side of the fabric.

Using the black pen transfer each design, outline shaping and placement marks onto the tracing paper. Choose a letter from the alphabet and trace onto the centre of the oval on the needlebook design. Centre each large design under a large square of silk aligning the placement marks with the straight grain and, using a lightbox or window if necessary, transfer the design only onto the wrong side of the fabric using the heat-soluble marker. Repeat with the small design and small square of silk.

Turn each piece of fabric over and re-position over the design. On the right side of the fabric, lightly mark the outline shaping. Work a line of tacking around the outline shaping on each piece using the silk sewing thread.

embroidery

See pages 118–119 for step-by-step instructions for working the bullion loop, bullion knot and interlaced chain stitch.

Refer to the close-up photograph for colour placement.

Use the no. 10 sharp needle for all bullion loops and knots, the no. 10 crewel for all other embroidery and the tapestry needle for the interlacing. Use the no. 8 and 10 crewel needles for construction as required.

ORDER OF WORK

SCISSOR SHEATH, PINWHEEL & NEEDLEBOOK

The bouquet and stripe embroidery design on each main piece is worked in the same manner. As the design is transferred onto the fabric using a minimum number of marks, it is important that the order of work is followed carefully.

The bullion loops and knots should be worked in the hand. Once these are complete on each piece, place the fabric into the appropriate hoop taking care to ensure that the lines are straight and the surface is taut. Work the remaining embroidery in the hoop.

BOUQUETS

Rose

At the marked position work a 10-wrap looped bullion using two strands of **E**. Using two strands of **D**, work three 12-wrap bullion knots around the centre (diag 1).

Work three 14-wrap bullion knots to cup the previous round and one 14-wrap bullion knot to cup the base of the three petals using two strands of **I** (diag 2).

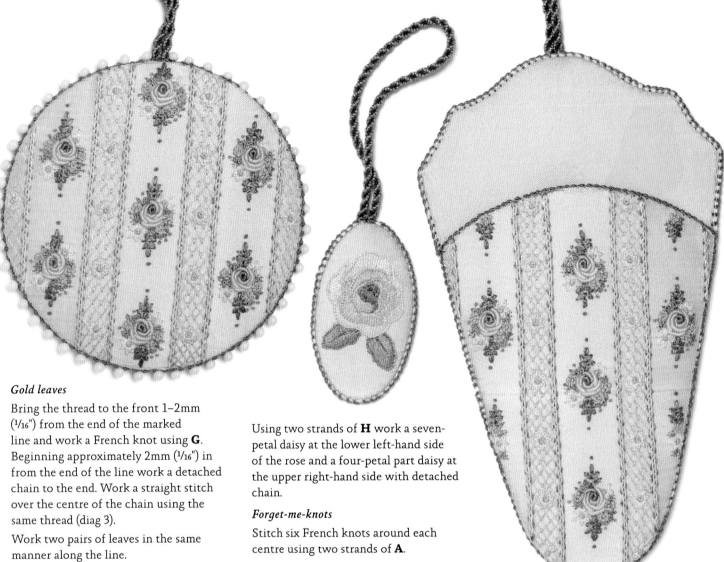

Gold leaves

Bring the thread to the front 1–2mm (¹⁄₁₆") from the end of the marked line and work a French knot using **G**. Beginning approximately 2mm (¹⁄₁₆") in from the end of the line work a detached chain to the end. Work a straight stitch over the centre of the chain using the same thread (diag 3).

Work two pairs of leaves in the same manner along the line.

Repeat at the remaining end of the line (diag 4).

White daisies

Using two strands of **C**, work a single wrap French knot for the centre of the forget-me-nots and a two-wrap knot for the daisies (diag 5).

Using two strands of **H** work a seven-petal daisy at the lower left-hand side of the rose and a four-petal part daisy at the upper right-hand side with detached chain.

Forget-me-knots

Stitch six French knots around each centre using two strands of **A**.

Foliage

Using **B**, work the foliage with detached chain and fly stitch (diag 6).

Violet flowers

Using **F**, work French knots at the positions indicated to complete the bouquet (diag 7).

STRIPES

Work a line of fine chain along each marked line using two strands of **H**. Work the interlacing down each line of chain with **G**. Using **F**, work back stitch down the centre of each line.

| Diag 3 | Diag 4 | Diag 5 | Diag 6 | Diag 7 |

The trellis couching is worked in two layers using **A**. Beginning at the top, work a diagonal straight stitch across one stripe at a 35° angle (diag 8).

Continue working parallel lines, 4mm (³/₁₆") apart down the length of the stripe. Complete any partial lines required at the upper and lower ends (diag 9).

Work a second set of parallel lines in the opposite direction, 4mm (³/₁₆") apart, intersecting the first to complete the first layer (diag 10).

Centering the stitches between those of the first layer, work a second layer of trellis with the straight stitches at the same angle as the first (diag 11).

Couch the intersecting lines in place down each side of the central diamonds (diag 12).

Using two strands of **C**, work French knots aligned with the centres of the bouquet rose down the length of each stripe. Surround each knot with seven detached chain petals using two strands of **H**.

MONOGRAM OVAL
(NEEDLEBOOK ONLY)

Oval

Stitch a line of chain around the oval using two strands of **H**, completing the line as shown (diag 13). Interlace the chain using two strands of **G** and work back stitch through the centre of the chain line using one strand of the same thread.

Monogram

Outline the letter with split stitch using **A**. Fill the shape with rows of running stitch padding, taking very small stitches into the fabric so that most of the thread sits on the top. Work a second layer of rows of running stitch padding, anchoring each stitch into the stitches beneath. Do not go through the fabric. Continue working layers, building up the padding, until the desired height is achieved. Using a new thread of **A**, cover the padding and outline with satin stitch.

Gold sprays

Using **G**, work a two-wrap French knot at the centre of the spray. Stitch the leaves in the same manner as the bouquets and finish with a single wrap French knot at each end. Work the second spray in the same manner.

SCISSOR FOB

The scissor fob is worked entirely in blanket stitch.

Rose

Work the centre of the rose using **E**, working the stitches close together to cover the fabric completely. Stitch the middle petals with **D**, leaving very small spaces between the stitches and the outer petals with **I**, leaving slightly larger spaces between the stitches.

Leaves

Stitch the leaves using **B**, keeping the stitches close together to cover the fabric completely.

TWISTED CORDS

Scissor sheath, pinwheel & needlebook

Each main element of the chatelaine requires a 40cm (16") length of twisted cord. This length is divided into one, 30cm (12") piece and one 10cm (4") piece.

The following instructions are for one long cord. Make three long cords.

Cut three 120cm (47") lengths of **J**. Knot the lengths together at each end. Secure one knotted end over a hook or sewing machine spool pin. Slip a pencil or thin dowel through the second knotted end. Twist the threads until the required tension is achieved. Hold the twisted threads at the centre and bring the ends together. Release the cord from the centre a little at a time until reaching the ends. Knot the ends together and trim away the original knots.

From the looped end of the cord, measure up 10cm (4") and mark with a pin. Using **G**, secure the thread into the cord just below the pin. Wrap the thread around the cord 5–6 times and secure the thread. Repeat just above the pin. Remove the pin and cut the cord between the two areas of binding. Put the short piece of cord aside. On the remaining piece, measure up 30cm (12") from the binding and mark with a pin. Using **G**, secure the thread into the cord just below the pin. Wrap the thread around the cord 5–6 times and secure the thread. Trim away the excess cord above the binding.

Scissor fob

The scissor fob requires a 15cm (6") length of twisted cord.

Make a twisted cord in the same manner as before using three, 45cm (18") lengths of **J**.

From the looped end measure up 15cm (6") and mark with a pin. Using **G**, secure the thread into the cord just below the pin. Wrap the thread around the cord 5–6 times and secure the thread. Trim away the excess cord above the binding.

construction.

See the liftout pattern.

BULLION KNOT

The distance from A to B is the length of the finished bullion knot.
To form a straight knot the number of wraps must cover this distance plus an extra 1–2 wraps.

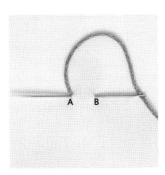

1 | Bring the needle to the front at A, and take the needle from B to A.

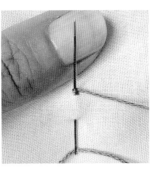

2 | Wrap the thread clockwise around the needle. Pull the wrap firmly down onto the fabric.

3 | Work the required number of wraps. Pack them down evenly as you wrap.

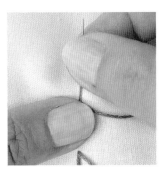

4 | Keeping tension on the wraps with the left thumb ease the needle through the fabric and wraps.

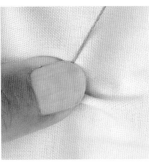

5 | Pull the thread, tugging it gently away from you all the way through.

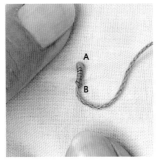

6 | Bring the thread towards you and the knot will lay back towards B.

7 | To ensure all the wraps are even, gently stroke and manipulate them with the needle while maintaining tension on the thread.

8 | Take the thread to the back at B and secure.

INTERLACED CHAIN STITCH

The addition of the undulating line of the interlacing stitch adds an elegant, lacy effect to a line of chain stitch

1 | Work a row of chain stitch.

2 | Change thread colour. Emerge at the top of the row.

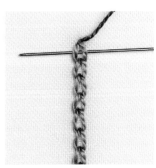

3 | Slide the needle, from right to left, under the first chain.

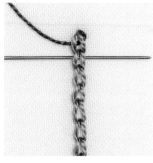

4 | Pull the thread through. Slide the needle from left to right under the next chain.

5 | Pull the thread through. Continue in this manner, alternating from side to side, to the end of the row.

6 | Take the thread to the back at the end of the row.

BULLION LOOP

A bullion loop is a variation of a bullion knot. It is formed in a similar manner, except that the distance between A and B is very short and the number of wraps is often large. Before anchoring the loop, take time to stroke and manipulate the wraps.

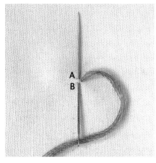

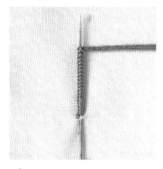

1 | Emerge at A and pull the thread through.

2 | Take the needle through the fabric from B to A, taking care not to split the thread. The thread is to the right of the needle.

3 | Raise the point of the needle and wrap the thread around it the required number of times.

4 | Holding the wraps firmly with your left thumb, begin to pull the needle and thread through the wraps.

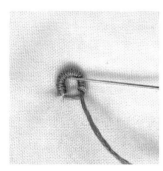

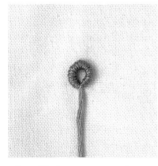

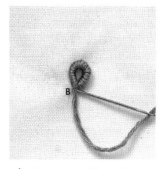

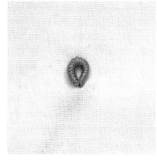

5 | Pull the thread all the way through. Using the needle, separate the wraps from the adjacent thread.

6 | Hold the wraps in place with your thumb (thumb not shown). Pull the thread towards you to tighten the wraps and curl them into a loop.

7 | Take the needle to the back at B to anchor the loop.

8 | Pull the thread through.

reticella sampler

before you begin

We recommend that you read the complete article

All embroidery is worked with ONE strand of thread

this design uses

Detached blanket stitch
Italian four-sided stitch
Needleweaving / Satin stitch
Venetian picots / Wrapping

The finished design measures 22cm x 11cm wide (8¾" x 4⅜").

requirements

FABRIC

35cm x 25cm wide (14" x 10") piece of 32-count antique white linen

SUPPLIES

Slate or scroll frame to fit fabric
Lacing thread
Contrasting sewing thread
Sharp embroidery scissors

NEEDLES

No. 9 crewel
No. 24 tapestry
No. 26 tapestry

THREADS & BEADS

DMC no. 80 cordonnet
A = ecru

DMC no. 8 perlé cotton
B = 712 cream

DMC no. 12 perlé cotton
C = 712 cream

preparation for embroidery

PREPARING THE FABRIC

Neaten the raw edges of the linen with a machine zigzag or overlock stitch to prevent fraying.

Using the sewing thread and a tapestry needle, mark the sampler panels with lines of tacking worked over and under two fabric threads. To begin, fold the linen in half down the length, finger press and tack along the line to mark the vertical centre. Repeat to mark the horizontal centre. Referring to the diagram, tack the outer rectangle and the panels as indicated (diag 1).

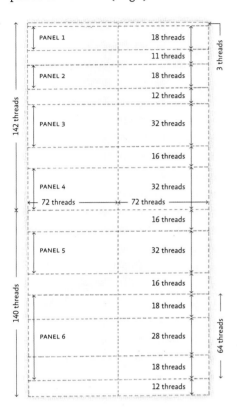

Attach the fabric to the frame ensuring that the surface is drum tight.

embroidery

See pages 128–129 for step-by-step instructions for working Italian four-sided stitch and Venetian picots.

Refer to the close-up photograph for stitch placement.

Use the no. 26 tapestry needle when working with the no. 12 perlé or no. 80 cordonnet and the no. 24 tapestry for the no. 8 perlé. Change to the crewel needle as required to pierce bars.

All embroidery is worked in the frame.

ORDER OF WORK

The needleweaving and needlelace fillings are all worked using **A**, and the surface embroidery using **B** and **C**. All picots are Venetian picots.

PANEL ONE

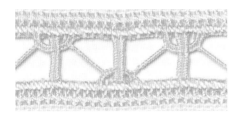

PREPARING THE CUTWORK PANEL

Inner border

A border of satin stitch outlines the cutwork area. Begin two fabric threads down from the upper tacked line of the panel. Using **B** and leaving five fabric threads at each side, work a row of satin stitch over three fabric threads. Using the same hole at the inner corner, stitch nine satin stitches down the first side of the panel. There will be two fabric stitches between the satin stitch and the side line of tacking (fig 1).

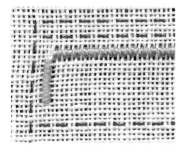

Continue to work satin stitch at the same spacing around the panel to complete the border.

Outer border

Italian four-sided stitch surrounds the inner border. Using **C** and beginning at the right-hand side of the panel, stitch Italian four-sided stitch over two x two fabric threads. The inner edge shares

holes with the outer edge of the satin stitch. Remove the tacking thread as you work (fig 2).

Cutting and removing threads

Mark a guide for the fabric threads to cut with a line of tacking along the horizontal centre of the panel in the following manner:

> Beginning at one side, go over nine threads and under four threads.
>
> Go over ten threads and under four threads eight times.
>
> Go over the remaining nine threads (fig 3).

Referring to the tacking and using the sharp scissors, cut and remove the vertical fabric threads for each section of nine and ten threads, cutting close to the satin stitch border. Cut and remove the horizonal fabric threads within the panel. Nine columns of four vertical fabric threads remain (fig 4).

NEEDLEWOVEN BARS

Using **A**, work needleweaving over each of the vertical fabric thread columns to create the bars. Begin with a waste knot below the first bar, to the outside of the four-sided stitch border. Carry the thread under the vertical threads and emerge on the outer edge of the satin stitch on the opposite edge of the panel

aligned with the centre of the vertical threads (fig 5).

With the carried thread to one side take it to the back at the centre of the vertical threads. From this point, weave over and under two fabric threads, incorporating the carried thread on one side to the base of the column, to create a needlewoven bar (diag 2).

Secure the thread on the wrong side under the border stitching. Work the second bar in a similar manner in the opposite direction, beginning with a waste knot above the panel and weaving upwards. Complete the remaining bars in the same manner, working in alternate directions.

Trim away the waste knots and thread tails.

ARCHES AND BARS FILLING

Begin the first arch by laying three foundation threads over which detached blanket stitch will be worked. Using **A**, begin with a waste knot and take the

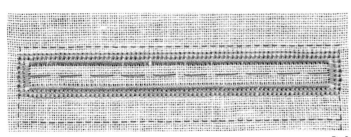

Fig 3

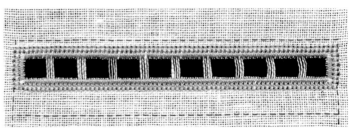

Fig 4

thread under the wrong side of a few four-sided stitches near the first woven bar. Emerge through the second fabric hole to the right of the bar (fig 6).

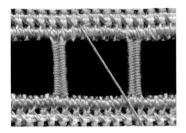

Carefully pass the needle and thread through the woven bar, 2mm (1/16") down from the satin stitch edge. To form the second half of the arch, anchor the thread through the second fabric hole to the left of the bar. Take the thread back to the right-hand side of the arch, passing through the woven bar, anchor the thread and return to the left-hand side in the same manner.

Work three detached blanket stitches over the foundation threads. To form the wrapped bar, take the thread to the lower left-hand corner and anchor through the inner corner hole of the four-sided stitch border (fig 7).

Wrap the bar back to the arch and work three detached blanket stitches before the woven bar. Weave the thread through the bar and cover the remaining half of the arch with six detached blanket stitches (fig 8).

Run the thread under the satin stitches on the wrong side to the third woven bar and leave.

Rotate the work 180°. Begin a new thread in the same manner as before, emerging two holes to the right of the second woven bar. Form a foundation in the same manner as before and work six detached blanket stitches. Weave across to the second half of the arch and work three stitches. Take the thread to the centre of the arch below and anchor the thread through the edge. Wrap the thread to return to the upper arch and work three more detached blanket stitches. Run the thread under the satin stitching on the wrong side to the fourth woven bar and leave.

Using the left threads, continue working detached blanket stitch arches and wrapped bars alternately across the upper and lower edges of the panel in the same manner, rotating the work as needed. Work the last bar from the lower right-hand corner to the arch, wrapping back to the corner.

Secure all threads under the border stitching on the wrong side. Trim any waste knots and all thread tails.

PANEL TWO

PREPARING THE CUTWORK PANEL

Prepare the cutwork panel and needlewoven bars in the same manner as panel one. After completing each woven bar, do not finish off the threads. Leave the tails so that they can be used for the picot arches.

Picot arches

Beginning at the upper end of the first woven bar, run the closest thread tail under the wrong side of the border stitching and emerge two fabric holes

to the left of the bar. Take the thread across to the right of the bar and back, in a similar manner to panel one, to make a foundation of two threads.

NOTE: Foundation threads for arches
Lay two threads when using thread left in reserve. When using a new thread, lay three threads.

Embroider two detached blanket stitches over the beginning of the foundation. Work a third stitch, adding a picot. Cover the remainder of the first half of the arch with two more detached blanket stitches. Weave the thread through the bar and embroider over the second half of the arch in the same manner as the first half.

NOTE: Each half of the arch is embellished with a picot at the midpoint. If you need to work more stitches to cover the arch, ensure that you work the picot when you reach the midpoint so that the picots are mirrored.

Continue working arches with picots alternately along the upper and lower ends of the woven bars across the panel, using the remaining thread tails. Finish off all thread tails on the wrong side of the work.

Wrapped bars

Beginning a new length of **A** with a waste knot, run the thread under the border stitching and emerge through the hole at the upper left-hand corner. Take the thread across to the opposite corner of the section and anchor through the fabric hole below the centre of the woven bar (fig 9).

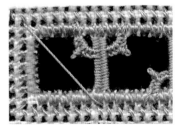

Return to the first corner and anchor the thread, forming a second foundation thread. Wrap the threads back to the second corner. Anchor the thread and work the bar in the second section from the lower left-hand corner to the upper right-hand corner. Continue working bars in the same manner across the panel, changing direction after each section.

> **HINT:** When you have insufficient thread to complete a wrapped bar, end off the thread after the previous bar and begin a new thread for the next. Do not change threads partway through a wrapped bar.

PANEL THREE

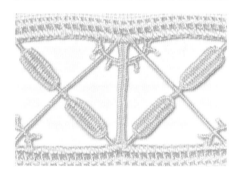

PREPARING THE CUTWORK PANEL

Inner and outer borders

Embroider the satin stitch and four-sided stitch borders in the same manner as before with **B** and **C**, using the tacked lines marking the panel as a guide.

Cutting and removing threads

Mark a guide for the fabric threads to cut with a line of tacking along the horizontal centre of the panel in the following manner:

> Beginning at one side, go over twenty-three threads and under four threads.
>
> Go over twenty-four and under four threads three times.
>
> Go over the remaining twenty-three threads.

Cut and remove the vertical fabric threads for each section of twenty-three and twenty-four threads. Cut and remove the horizonal fabric threads.

Four columns of four vertical fabric threads remain.

NEEDLEWOVEN BARS

Using **A**, work needleweaving over each of the vertical fabric thread columns in the same manner as panel one.

WRAPPED BARS

These are worked in a similar manner to panel two, with wrapping worked over two threads for each bar. Lay the threads and wrap one bar completely in each section, in the same manner as panel two, before commencing the second bar in each section.

When laying the threads for the second bar, the thread is taken through the completed wrapped bar. Change to the crewel needle to carefully pierce the completed bar at the centre (fig 10).

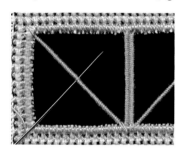

> **HINT:** When piercing the bar begin with the needle held vertically to the bar. Push the needle tip into the bar, then rotate the needle until it is horizontal and push through the bar.

Wrap the second bar, taking the thread under the completed bar at the centre.

PICOT ARCHES

Referring to the close-up photograph, lay threads for the arches in a similar manner to panels one and two, laying two threads if using reserved thread tails or three threads if using a new thread. Pierce the wrapped bars and weave through the woven bar 3mm (⅛") from the edge of the satin stitch.

Embroider detached blanket stitch over the arches, working two stitches, a stitch with a picot and two more stitches for each section. When reaching a wrapped bar, take the thread under the bar and

continue stitching on the other side. For a woven bar, weave the thread through.

After each arch, finish off the thread under the border on the wrong side of the work.

NEEDLEWOVEN LOZENGES

The lozenges are worked over the wrapped bars that are not connected to arches. For lozenges of equal size, use the same spacing from each end of the wrapped bar half.

Knot the end of a length of **A** in the crewel needle. Count in three wraps from the inner end of a wrapped bar half and pierce the bar (fig 11).

Carefully pull the thread through until the knot is against the bar. Pierce the bar three wraps from the opposite end, taking the needle in the opposite direction (fig 12).

Pull the thread through to create half an oval shape. Repeat in in the opposite direction for the second half of the oval (fig 13).

Repeat three more times, so that a framework is formed from two and a half rounds of thread, ending at the outer end (fig 14).

Fill the lozenge with needleweaving, working over the framework and wrapped bar from the outer end (fig 15).

When the needleweaving is complete, carefully cut away the knot. To finish the thread, slide the needle under the woven threads on the wrong side of the lozenge from one end to the other, pull the thread through and carefully trim the tail close to the weaving.

PANEL FOUR

PREPARING THE CUTWORK PANEL

Prepare the cutwork panel, needlewoven bars and wrapped bars in the same manner as panel three. Leave any long thread tails in reserve.

CORNER FILLING

The three leaves each have a wrapped bar foundation and are small lozenges, worked in the same manner as panel two.

Foundation

Additional wrapped bars are added to the corners. Using a reserved or new thread, emerge through the fifth fabric hole to the left of a woven bar at the the top of the panel. Pierce the diagonal wrapped bar below and carefully pull the thread through (fig 16).

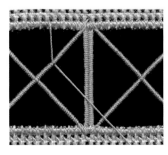

Weave the thread through the woven bar directly across from this point,

and pierce the next wrapped bar, maintaining the straight line (fig 17).

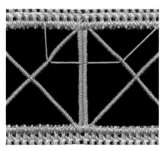

Pull the thread through and anchor it through the fifth hole to the right of the woven bar (fig 18).

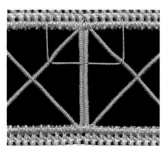

Return the thread to the left-hand side, following the thread path in reverse. Wrap the two threads, beginning at the upper left-hand edge. Take the thread under the diagonal wrapped bar and continue wrapping to the woven bar (fig 19).

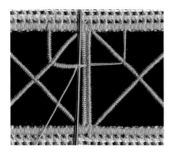

Take the thread under the woven bar and continue wrapping the remaining two sections in the same manner. Leave any remaining thread in reserve for working wrapped bars further along the panel.

Needlewoven leaves

Work the leaf over the vertical bar first. Knot the end of a length of **A** and work an oval framework around the bar, piercing the bar at the upper and lower ends. Begin at the lower end and take the thread around two and a half times, finishing at the upper end (fig 20).

Fill the leaf with needleweaving, working from the upper end. Take the thread under the intersection and work the horizontal leaf in the same manner, followed by the diagonal leaf. Repeat across the panel. Turn the work and repeat for the second side.

Work the wrapped bar foundations and leaves at each end of the panel, spacing the foundation threads at the border five fabric holes from a corner.

CENTRE FILLING

Use a new length of **A** with a knot in the end. Working in a clockwise direction and piercing each of the four diagonal bars 3mm (⅛") from the intersection, take the thread in a circle around the centre of a panel twice. Take the thread through the next bar on from the knotted tail (fig 21).

Take the thread over and around the next bar and begin to cover the threads with detached blanket stitch. To begin, work three stitches, a picot with the fourth stitch, followed by three more stitches (fig 22).

Take the thread under the next diagonal bar and repeat the stitch pattern around the circle, cutting away the waste knot as you work past it.

To finish off the thread, connect the last stitch with the first and run the thread under the wrong side of three blanket stitches. Trim the tail close to the stitching. Repeat at the centre of each panel section.

PANEL FIVE

PREPARING THE CUTWORK PANEL

Prepare the cutwork panel, needlewoven bars and wrapped bars in the same manner as panel three. Add a vertical wrapped bar from the centre of the upper edge to the centre of the lower edge of each section. Work a long wrapped bar through the horizontal centre of the panel, linking all the squares. When laying the foundation, pierce the wrapped bar intersections and weave through the woven bars.

PICOT ARCHES

Using reserved or new threads, work picot arches in the same manner as panel three at the upper and lower end of each woven bar, and in each corner of the panel. Work picot arches at each end of the horizontal and vertical wrapped bars in a similar manner to the corner arches.

NOTE: To avoid tangled threads from numerous long thread tails, you can begin to embroider the arches as you complete the required wrapped bars, rather than working all the wrapped bars before beginning the arches.

PICOT CIRCLES

Work the circles after the wrapped bars and arches are complete. Embroider a detached blanket stitch circle with picots at the centre of each intersection in a similar manner to panel four, adding a picot to the midpoint of each section.

PANEL SIX

PREPARING THE CUTWORK AREAS

This panel has three sections.

Inner and outer borders

Following the tacked guidelines, embroider the inner border of the upper and lower sections of eighteen fabric stitches in the same manner as panel one. Work the inner border of the centre section in a similar manner to panel three, leaving two fabric threads between the satin stitch borders. Surround the entire panel with four-sided stitch and work a row of four-sided stitch between the sections.

UPPER AND LOWER SECTIONS

Needlewoven bars

Remove threads and work the needlewoven bars in the same manner as panel one.

Filling

Complete each section before moving on to the next.

Beginning in the upper left-hand corner, take the thread to the lower right-hand corner and back. Wrap to the centre of the bar. At this point, take the thread to the lower left-hand corner, across to the upper right-hand corner and back to the lower left-hand corner (fig 23).

Wrap to the centre. Take the thread back to the lower right-hand corner. Wrap to

the centre (fig 24).

Weave around the centre in a counter-clockwise direction, over, under, over, under, three times. When reaching the unwrapped bar on the third round, wrap the threads to the edge of the satin stitch border (fig 25).

If the thread is long enough to complete the next section, run the thread under the wrong side of the woven bar to the lower edge. Work the next section as a mirror image to the first, beginning and ending at the lower edge. If needed, finish off the first thread and begin a new one under the wrong side of the border stitching. Continue across the section in the same manner, working alternately from the upper or lower edge.

CENTRE SECTION

Complete this section in the same manner as panel five.

SATIN STITCH

All satin stitch is embroidered using **B** after all cutwork panels are complete.

ROW 1

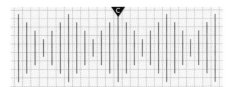

Referring to chart one, embroider satin stitch diamonds across the area between panels two and three. The stitching is centred horizontally within the space. The row begins and ends with the longest stitch of a diamond aligned with the outer edge of the four-sided stitch border.

ROW 2

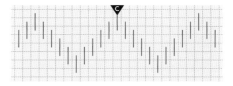

Referring to chart two, embroider a zigzag line of satin stitch across the area between panels three and four. The stitching is centred horizontally within the panel, with the peak of each zigzag four fabric threads below the four-sided stitch border of panel three. The line begins at the left-hand side with the second stitch before a peak, and ends with the second stitch after a peak.

ROW 3

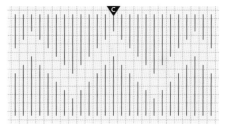

Referring to chart three, embroider sawtooth satin stitch in two rows across the area between panels four and five. The outer edge of the rows are two fabric threads from the four-sided stitch borders of panels four and five. The zigzag void is aligned with the zigzag satin stitch above panel four.

ROWS 4 AND 5

Embroider saw tooth satin stitch above panel six in the same manner as the lower edge of row 3. Work a mirror image row below panel six.

ITALIAN FOUR-SIDED STITCH

This stitch can be worked in several different ways to achieve the same result. Here, it is worked from the right side and from right to left. It can be worked with the fabric in the hand, rather than a hoop or frame, so that the stitches can be worked in a scooping motion. If the fabric is held taut, follow the thread path and use a stabbing motion with the needle.

1 | Emerge at A and take the needle from B to C.

2 | Pull the thread taut. Take the needle from B to D.

3 | Pull the thread taut. Take the needle from A to D.

4 | Pull the thread taut. Take the needle from C to E.

5 | Pull the thread taut. Take the needle from C to F.

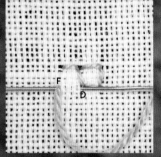

6 | Pull the thread taut. Take the needle from D to F.

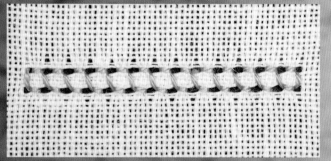

7 | Pull the thread taut. Continue the stitching sequence to complete the row.

VENETIAN PICOT

A delicate feature of reticella needlelace, Venetian picots are added at midpoints around blanket stitch arches and circles in the sampler. Originally worked using a horse hair to tension the picot loop, a length of sewing thread is an accessible substitute that enables a fine picot to be created. Embroider detached blanket stitches from left to right over the foundation threads to the position for a picot. The loop of the picot should be just large enough to fit two blanket stitches.

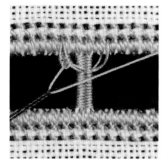

1 | At the position for a picot, place a length of sewing thread over the working thread.

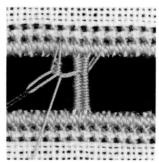

2 | Take the needle over the foundation threads and pull through.

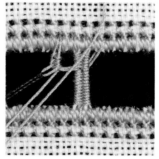

3 | Holding the sewing thread, tension the loop and the working thread. Draw down the working thread to adjust the loop size.

4 | Loop the working thread as shown and hold in place (not shown).

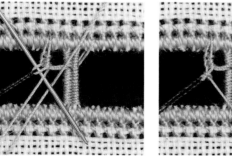

5 | Take the needle under the first three threads and over the working thread to begin a blanket stitch.

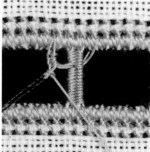

6 | Pull the thread taut, ensuring it is as close to the tip of the loop as possible.

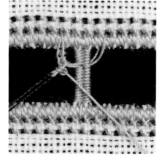

7 | Work a second blanket stitch beside the first.

8 | Remove the sewing thread. Continue working blanket stitch over the foundation.

winter sunset

before you begin

We recommend that you read the complete article

See the liftout pattern for the embroidery design

All embroidery is worked with TWO strands of thread unless specified

this design uses

Blanket stitch / Bullion knot
Chain stitch / Colonial knot
Coral stitch / French knot
Ghiordes knot
Heavy chain stitch
Layered blanket stitch
Ladder stitch
Long and short stitch
Outline stitch / Pistil stitch
Satin stitch / Split stitch
Stem stitch / Straight stitch
Trellis couching
Weaving / Wheatear stitch
Whipped chain variation
Woven ladder stitch
Woven raised chain stitch
Woven spider web

The finished footstool top measures 27cm (10⅝") square.

requirements

FABRIC

40cm (16") square of natural linen/cotton blend
40cm (16") square of white cotton voile

SUPPLIES

28.5 cm (11¼") square footstool base with 27cm (10⅝") upholstered pad (optional)
1.2m x 6mm (1yd 12" x ¼") braid (optional)
40cm (16") stretcher bars
Thumb tacks
Fine black pen
Tracing paper
Fine heat-soluble fabric marker

NEEDLES

No. 7 crewel
No. 8 crewel
No. 10 crewel
No. 26 tapestry

THREADS

DMC no. 12 perlé cotton
A = 356 med terracotta
B = 644 med beige-grey
C = 778 vy lt antique mauve
D = 822 lt beige-grey
E = 927 lt grey-green

DMC stranded cotton
F = 437 lt tan
G = 451 dk shell grey
H = 452 med shell grey
I = 524 vy lt fern green
J = 632 vy dk mocha
K = 644 med beige-grey
L = 738 vy lt tan (2)
M = 739 ultra lt tan
N = 778 vy lt antique mauve
O = 779 dk cocoa
P = 822 lt beige-grey
Q = 924 vy dk grey-green
R = 926 med grey-green
S = 927 lt grey-green
T = 950 vy lt mocha
U = 3051 dk green-grey
V = 3052 med green-grey (2)
W = 3053 green-grey
X = 3782 lt French grey
Y = 3857 dk rosewood (2)
Z = 3858 med rosewood
AA = 3859 lt rosewood

preparation for embroidery

PREPARING THE FABRICS

Press the squares of linen/cotton blend and white cotton voile and check to ensure that they are the same size. Trim if necessary.

TRANSFERRING THE DESIGN

Using the black pen trace the embroidery design and placement marks onto the tracing paper. Tape the tracing to a lightbox or window. Centre the linen/cotton blend over the tracing aligning the placement marks with the straight grain and tape in place. Transfer the design using the heat-soluble marker.

With the design uppermost place the square of linen/cotton blend over the square of white cotton voile aligning the edges and pin the fabrics together. Using a machine zigzag or overlock stitch, stitch the fabrics together around the outer edge. Attach the fabrics to the stretcher bars using the thumb tacks ensuring that the surface is taut.

embroidery

See page 138 for the weaving patterns and pages 137–141 for step-by-step instructions for working Ghiordes knot, ladder stitch, layered blanket stitch, woven ladder stitch and woven raised chain stitch.

Refer to the close-up photograph for colour placement.

Use the no. 7 crewel needle for working the warp threads in the weaving, the no. 7 and 8 crewel needles with two strands of stranded cotton, the no. 10 crewel with one strand of stranded cotton and the no. 26 tapestry needle for the whipping and the weft threads in the weaving.

All embroidery is worked in the frame.

ORDER OF WORK

MAIN STEM

Stem

The main stem is worked with four rows of whipped chain variation. In some parts of the stem the rows are close together and in other sections they are further apart.

Using **J** work a line of chain stitch along the right-hand side of each stem section. Whip the outer side only of each line of chain with one strand of **Y** (diag 1).

Working to ensure that the stitches are aligned with the first row, stitch a second line of chain stitch next to the first on each stem section using **J**. Using one strand of **Y**, whip the adjacent edges of the first and second rows together (diag 2).

Work two more rows of whipped chain in the same manner as the second row using the same threads. To complete the stem whip the outer edge of the last row of chain using one strand of **Y**.

Tendrils

Using the photograph as a guide to colour placement work the stem tendrils in coral stitch using **Q** and **R**.

LEAVES ON MAIN STEM

There are three leaves worked on the main stem all worked in the same manner.

Using one strand of thread fill the main area of each leaf with weaving pattern 1 using **D** for colour 1 and **E** for colour 2. Once the weaving is complete and using **V**, weave along each side of the colour 1 blocks in both directions following the pattern for colour 1.

131

The upper edge and vein on each leaf are worked in the same manner. Using **L** work wheatear stitch between the lines of each section. When turning corners work an extra side stitch into the space that is created (diag 3).

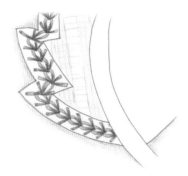

Work a French knot into the loop created at the centre of the stitch using **O**. Outline each section with heavy chain stitch using the same thread. Using **V** outline the remaining half of each leaf with heavy chain stitch. Using one strand of **U** work outline stitch along the outside of the heavy chain stitch.

FLOWER 1

Petals

At the centre of each circle work a woven spider web using **Z**. Stitch seven straight stitch spokes to the centre. Bring the thread to the front close to the centre and begin weaving under and over the spokes. Pull the thread quite firmly for the first 2–3 rounds to ensure that the centre is covered. Continue weaving until the circle is full. Using one strand of **Y** work a circle of fine chain stitch around the centre. Working slightly larger chain stitches and beginning adjacent to the centre, work two rows using **N**, then **T** and finishing with **P**.

Fill the remaining space between the circles with outline stitch using one strand of **AA**. Work back and forth in each small area keeping the rows close together until each section is full. Using one strand of **Y** outline the edge of each circle with outline stitch.

Border

Using **V** and beginning at the base work ladder stitch along the inner curved lines along each side of the flower. Beginning on the inner edge of one curved section and using one strand of **B**, weave under and over the rungs of the ladder. Take the needle to the back in the valley at the end of each curved section. Bring the thread to the front close to the end of the previous row and weave back along the section. Take the needle to the back in the valley. Continue working rows in this manner until the curved section is complete. Work the remaining sections in the same manner. Work a bullion knot in the valley over the ends of each section using **V**. Outline the outer curved edge with outline stitch using one strand of **U**.

> **NOTE:** You may find that when working ladder stitch around curves that the outer, plaited edge of the ladder stitch pulls in, exposing the ends of the rib stitches. This creates a pretty effect on the edge but to prevent it from happening, relax your stitch tension a little.

Using **Y** outline the inner edge adjacent to the circles with outline stitch.

Pad the three leaves at the tip of the flower with horizontal rows of satin stitch using **X**. Cover each leaf with long and short stitch using one strand and beginning at the base with **N** and shading through **L**, **M** to **W** at the leaf tip. Outline each leaf and the circle with outline stitch using one strand of **Y**. Fill the circle with close horizontal rows of Ghiordes knot using **Y**. Clip and comb the knots until you have a rich, plush surface.

Centre

Using three strands of **L** work long horizontal straight stitches 3mm (⅛") apart to fill the shape. Using the same thread and following the step-by-step, work raised chain stitch using the straight stitches as a foundation. Weave between the rows of raised chain stitch using three strands of **O**. Work a split stitch outline along the upper edges of the shape using **O**.

Calyx

Pad the calyx with horizontal straight stitches using **X**. Cover the padding with long and short stitch using one strand and beginning at the base with **V** and shading through **W**, **N**, **L** to **M** at the tip. Using one strand of **U** work trellis couching over the shape working the long straight stitches and the couching with the same thread. Work outline stitch around the calyx with one strand of **U**.

Detached petals

Pad each petal with horizontal satin stitch using **X**. Work long and short stitch with one strand over the padding, beginning at the base with **R** and shading through **S**, **W** to **K** at the tip.

Using one strand of **Q** work outline stitch beginning at the centre of the base and working along the inner edge. From the tip work one stitch down the outer edge.

FRUIT 1

Rind

Using one strand fill the rind with weaving pattern 2 using **D** for colour 1 and **A** for colour 2. Once the weaving is complete weave on each side of the colour 1 blocks in both directions using **Y** and following the pattern for colour 1.

Once the leaves at the tip are complete outline the outer edge of the rind with outline stitch using one strand of **Y**.

Seeds

Using one strand of **G** work a line of fine chain stitch around the oval centre of each seed. Fill the outer area of each seed with rows of larger chain stitches working two rounds using **L** and two rounds using **M**.

Fill the remaining area between the seeds with rows of outline stitch using one strand of **N**, working back and forth in each small area until full. Using one strand of **U** outline each seed with outline stitch. Fill the centre of each seed with close horizontal rows of Ghiordes knot using **G**. Clip and comb the knots until you have a rich, plush surface.

Inner rind edge

Pad the edge area with rows of stem stitch using **Z**. With one strand of **Z** work blanket stitch over the padding with the bead along the inner edge. Using one strand of **Y** work a line of outline stitch in the ditch between the woven rind and the edge of the blanket stitch.

Large base leaves

Using three strands of **AA** work long horizontal straight stitches 3mm (⅛") apart over the inner area of each leaf. Using the same thread work raised chain stitch using the straight stitches as a foundation. Using three strands of **T** weave between the rows of raised chain stitch. Omitting the dark area at the tip of one leaf, work chain stitch around the inner area on each leaf using **V**.

Continue working rows of chain using **W**, adding part rows where the shape widens. Using **P** work a row of chain stitch along the outer edge of each leaf. Using **K** work complete and incomplete rows of chain stitch over any space remaining between the rows of **W** and **P**.

Pad the small dark section at one leaf tip with vertical rows of stem stitch using **U**. With one strand of the same thread work blanket stitch over the padding ensuring that the bead is on the outer edge.

Work around the outer edge of each leaf with outline stitch using one strand of **U**. With the same thread work outline

stitch in the ditch between the centre and outer edge of each leaf.

Sepals

Fill the sepals above the leaves with stem stitch padding using **X**. Work long and short stitch with one strand of thread over the padding beginning at the base on the right-hand sepal with **W** and shading through **N**, **T** to **P** at the tips. On the left-hand side begin at the base with **V** and shade through **W**, **N**, **T** to **P** at the tips. Referring to the photograph for placement and using one strand of **U** for both the long stitches and couching, work areas of trellis couching over the sepals. Using the same thread work outline stitch around each sepal.

Small tip leaves

Work long and short stitch on the left-hand side of each leaf beginning at the centre vein with **W** and working the outer edge with **T**.

Fill the remaining half of each leaf with chain stitch using the photograph as a guide to colour placement. Begin with **V** adjacent to the vein and change to **W** then **K** and finish with **P**.

Stitch the vein and right-hand outline with outline stitch using one strand of **U**. Work outline stitch along the remaining edge using one strand of **Z**.

Outline the area at the base of the leaves with chain stitch using one strand of **Y**. Fill the area with close horizontal rows of Ghiordes knots using **Y**. Clip and comb the knots until you have a rich, plush surface.

FLOWER 2

Upper petals

Each petal is worked in the same manner. Using three strands of thread work long horizontal straight stitches 3mm (1/8") apart over each petal.

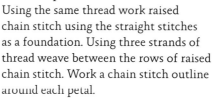

Using the same thread work raised chain stitch using the straight stitches as a foundation. Using three strands of thread weave between the rows of raised chain stitch. Work a chain stitch outline around each petal.

Use the chart to determine the colours to use for each petal.

Stamens

Using **AA** work a line of heavy chain stitch along each stamen. Work outline stitch along the inside curve using one strand of **Y**. Stitch seven French knots around each tip using **P**. Using the photograph as a guide work straight stitches fanning around the tip between the French knots using one strand of **Y**.

Lower petals

Fill the inner area of each petal with weaving pattern 3 using **D** for colour 1 and **C** for colour 2.

The outer area of each petal is filled with rows of chain stitch. Add part rows of chain stitch where necessary to fill the wider sections. Begin working

around the inner leaf section with one row of chain using **V**. On the lower line continue the row of chain along the curl at the tip of the petal. Continue working rows and part rows where necessary using **W**, **L** and **M** on the outer edge.

Using one strand of **U** work a row of outline stitch in the ditch between the inner and outer petal sections. Using the same thread work outline stitch around the outer edge of each petal.

FLOWER 3

Leaves

Fill the inner half of each leaf with long and short stitch using one strand of thread. Begin at the base with **W** and work diagonally down the leaf shading into **T** and **P** at the widest point. Once the outer half of each leaf is complete work outline stitch down the vein and around the outer edge of the inner half using one strand of **Y**.

On the outer half of each leaf work a line of chain stitch on each of the curved lines. Work outline stitch along the lower edge of each row of chain stitch. Stitch evenly spaced French knots in the space between the stitched lines. Work outline stitch around the outer edge of the section with one strand of **U**.

FLOWER 2

	Raised chain stitch 3 strands	Weaving 3 strands	Outline 2 strands
Left petal	**M**	**H**	**O**
Centre petal	**L**	**G**	**O**
Right petal	**F**	**O**	**O**

FLOWER 3

		Chain stitch 2 strands	Outline stitch 1 strand	French knots 2 strands
Right side leaf	**V** 4 lines	**U**	**Z**
	W 4 lines	**V**	**Z**, **AA** 1 strand of each
	I 3 lines	**W**	**AA**
Left side leaf	**V** 3 lines	**U**	**Z**
	W 4 lines	**V**	**Z**, **AA** 1 strand of each
	I 2 lines	**W**	**AA**

Use the chart to determine the colours to use for the outer half of each leaf.

Petals

PETALS 1, 4 AND 8

Fill the inner section of petals 1 and 8 and all of petal 4 with weaving pattern 2 using **D** for colour 1 and **A** for colour 2. Once the weaving is complete and using **Y**, weave along each side of the colour 1 blocks in both directions following the pattern for colour 1. Pad the outer border of petals 1 and 8 with stem stitch using **Z**. Using one strand of the same thread work blanket stitch over the padding with the bead on the outer edge. Work a line of outline stitch in the ditch between the blanket stitch and weaving, continuing down to the base of the petal using one strand of **Y**.

Once all the petals are complete work a line of outline stitch around petal 4 using one strand of **Y**.

PETALS 2 AND 7

Work these petals in the same manner as the large base leaves on Fruit 1.

PETALS 3 AND 6

Pad the inner section of each petal with stem stitch using **X**. Work long and short stitch with one strand of thread over the padding beginning at the base with **N** and shading to **T** at the tip.

Stitching from the inner edge of the outer section work layered blanket stitch to fill the area. Working so that each ridge is on a line, begin with **V** changing to **W** then **K** and finishing with **P** on the upper edge. Using **W** work a pistil stitch between the stitches on the final row. Bring the thread to the surface next to the penultimate row and extend the stitch outside the ridge of the last row (diag **4**).

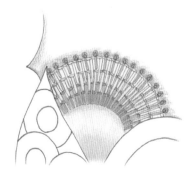

Work a row of outline stitch in the ditch between the inner and outer sections using one strand of **U**.

PETAL 5

Using one strand of **G** work a line of fine chain stitch around each oval centre. Fill the outer area with rows of larger chain stitches using one strand of thread and working two rounds using **L** and two rounds using **M**.

Fill the remaining area between the ovals with rows of outline stitch using one strand of **N** and working back and forth in each small area until full. Using one strand of **U** outline each oval with outline stitch. Fill each oval centre with close horizontal rows of Ghiordes knot using **G**. Clip and comb the knots until you have a rich, plush surface. Work outline stitch around the shape using one strand of **Y**.

Calyx

Pad the upper section with horizontal straight stitches using **X**. Work long and short stitch over the padding with one strand of thread beginning with **AA** at the base and shading through **N**, **T** and **M** to **I** at the tip.

Using the photograph as a guide to stitch placement work trellis couching over the lower section using one strand of **Z** for both the long straight stitches and couching. Work outline stitch around the upper section omitting the area where the upper section meets the lower section using one strand of **Y**.

Outline the lower section with fine chain stitch using one strand of **Y**. Fill the area with close horizontal rows of Ghiordes knot using **Y**. Clip and comb the knots until you have a rich, plush surface.

FLOWER 4

Petals

At the centre of each circle work a woven spider web using **Z** in the same manner as Flower 1.

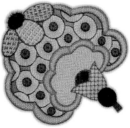

Using one strand of **Y** work a circle

of fine chain stitch around the centre. Working slightly larger chain stitches and beginning adjacent to the centre, work two rows using **N**, then **T** and finishing with **P**.

Fill the remaining space between the circles with outline stitch using one strand of **AA**. Work back and forth in each small area keeping the rows close together until each section is full. Using one strand of **Y** outline the edge of each circle with outline stitch.

Fill the scalloped area at the base of the petals with weaving pattern 4 using **D** for colour 1 and **C** for colour 2.

Border

Using **V** and beginning at the base work ladder stitch along each side of the flower and around the scalloped shape at the base of the petals. Beginning on the inner edge of one curved section and using one strand of **B**, weave under and over the rungs of the ladder. Take the needle to the back in the valley at the end of each curved section. Bring the thread to the front close to the end of the previous row and weave back along the section. Take the needle to the back in the valley. Continue working rows in this manner until the curved section is complete. Work the remaining sections in the same manner. Work a bullion knot in the valley over the ends of each section using **V**. Outline the outer edge of the woven ladder stitch with outline stitch using one strand of **U**. Using the same thread outline the inner edge of the scalloped shape at the base with outline stitch. Using **Y** outline the inner edge adjacent to the circles with outline stitch.

Calyx

Pad the centre section of the calyx with horizontal satin stitch using **X**. Cover the padding with long and short stitch using one strand of thread and beginning at the base with **W** and shading through **N** to **L** at the tips. Work trellis couching over the shape using one strand of **U** for the long straight stitches and couching.

Outline the semi-circle at the top of the calyx with fine chain stitch using one strand of **G**.

Fill the area with close horizontal rows of Ghiordes knot using **G**. Clip and comb the knots until you have a rich, plush surface.

Using one strand of **O** work a row of outline stitch in the ditch between the weaving and the chain stitch edge. Work outline stitch around the centre section of the calyx with one strand of **U**.

Outline the circle at the base of the calyx with fine chain stitch using one strand of **Y**. Fill the area with close horizontal rows of Ghiordes knot using **Y**. Clip and comb the knots until you have a rich, plush surface.

Upper petals

Using three strands of **M** for the centre petal and three strands of **L** for the side petals work long horizontal straight stitches 3mm (1/8") apart. Using the same thread work raised chain stitch over the straight stitch foundation. Weave between the rows of raised chain stitch using three strands of **H** for the centre petal and **G** for the side petals. Work split stitch around each petal using **O**.

Outline the centre of the petals with fine chain stitch using one strand of **Y**. Fill the area with close horizontal rows of Ghiordes knot using **Y**. Clip and comb the knots until you have a rich, plush surface. Work six colonial knots around the outer edge of the centre using **W**.

Detached petals

Pad all the petals with horizontal satin stitch using **X**. Work long and short stitch with one strand over the padding, beginning at the base with **N** and shading through **L** to **I** for the three upper petals and beginning with **R** and shading through **S**, **W** and **K** on the four side petals.

Work outline stitch around each upper petal with one strand of **Y**. Using one strand of **Q** work outline stitch beginning at the centre of the base and working along the inner edge. From the tip work one stitch down the outer edge.

SMALL FLOWERS

There are five, small, three-petal flowers in the design. Each one is worked in the same manner with variation used in the petal colours.

Calyx

Pad the calyx of each flower with horizontal straight stitch using **X**. Work long and short stitch over the padding with one strand of thread beginning with **V** at the base and shading through **W** to **I** at the tips. Using the photograph as a guide to stitch placement work trellis couching over the base of each calyx using one strand of **U** for both the long straight stitches and couching.

Once the petals are complete work outline stitch around the calyx using the same thread.

Petals

Pad the centre petal only with horizontal straight stitches using one strand of **X**.

Fill all the petals with long and short stitch beginning at the base on the grey flowers with **G** and shading through **H** and **M** to **I** and beginning at the base on the pink flowers with **N** and shading through **L** and **M** to **I**.

Work outline stitch around the grey petals using one strand of **O** and around the pink petals using one strand of **Z**.

Stem

Using **O** work a line of chain stitch along the inside curve. Work a line of split stitch along the outside curve using **G** and a line of outline stitch on the outer edge of the split stitch using one strand of **O**.

Tendrils

Work the tendrils in the same manner as the main stem tendrils.

construction

The finished embroidery can be made into a cushion or footstool as shown here. Take your embroidery and footstool base to an upholsterer to have it made up. The braid is applied to conceal the join between the wooden base and embroidered top or can be used to edge a cushion.

GHIORDES KNOT

This stitch is excellent for creating raised areas of tufting. Work horizontal rows to fill the required shape.

1 | Leaving a tail, take the thread to the back at A. Emerge at B then take the needle to the back at C.

2 | Pull the thread through. Re-emerge at A and tighten the first stitch. Take the needle to the back at D.

3 | Pull the thread through leaving a loop. Re-emerge at C and take the needle to the back at E.

4 | Re-emerge at D and tighten the stitch to secure the previous loop. Leaving a loop, take the needle to the back at F.

5 | Repeat steps 3 and 4 to the end of the row. After the last stitch, trim the tail level with the loops.

6 | Continue stitching rows to fill the shape. Hold the loops upright and trim, not too short.

7 | Comb the cut threads to separate the plies. Continue combing and trimming until the desired effect is achieved.

needleweaving patterns

Read the hints on the facing page before beginning. The diagrams shoulds be read from right to left.

O = over   **U** = under

PATTERN ONE

Warp:
6 x colour 1
6 x colour 2

Weft:
6 x colour 1
6 x colour 2

Pattern repeat is 12 rows

Colour 1	**Colour 2**
Row 1 O2, U2	Row 7 (U2) O2, U2
Row 2 O2, U2	Row 8 (U2) O2, U2
Row 3 (U2) O2, U2	Row 9 O2, U2
Row 4 (U2) O2, U2	Row 10 O2, U2
Row 5 O2, U2	Row 11 (U2) O2, U2
Row 6 O2, U2	Row 12 (U2) O2, U2

PATTERN TWO

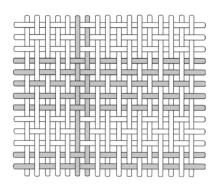

Warp:
10 x colour 1
2 x colour 2

Weft:
5 x colour 2
3 x colour 1

Pattern repeat is 8 rows

Colour 1	**Colour 2**
Row 1 (U1) O1, U2	Row 4 (U2) O1, U2
Row 2 O1, U2	Row 5 O1, U1
Row 3 (U1) O1, U2	Row 6 (U1) O1, U1
	Row 7 O1, U1
	Row 8 (U2) O1, U2

PATTERN THREE

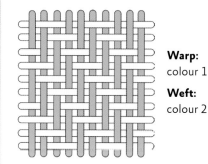

Warp:
colour 1

Weft:
colour 2

Pattern repeat is 4 rows

Row 1 (O1, U2) O2, U2
Row 2 (U2) O2, U2
Row 3 (U1) O2, U2
Row 4 O2, U2

PATTERN FOUR

Warp:
colour 1

Weft:
colour 2

Pattern repeat is 16 rows

Row 1 (O1, U2) O2, U2	Row 9 (O1, U2) O2, U2
Row 2 O2, U2	Row 10 (U2) O2, U2
Row 3 (U1) O2, U2	Row 11 (U1) O2, U2
Row 4 (U2) O2, U2	Row 12 O2, U2
Row 5 (O1, U2) O2, U2	Row 13 (O1, U2) O2, U2
Row 6 O2, U2	Row 14 (U2) O2, U2
Row 7 (U1) O2, U2	Row 15 (U1) O2, U2
Row 8 (U2) O2, U2	Row 16 O2, U2

LAYERED BLANKET STITCH

A striped band is created with layers of blanket stitch. Variations can be made by altering the length of the stitches and colour combinations. Hazel has chosen soft shades to create a gentle fade towards the outer edge of the band.

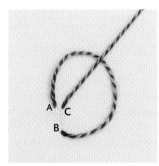

1 | First row. Emerge at A. Take the thread to the back at B leaving a loop and emerge through the loop at C.

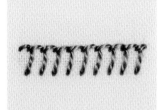

2 | Pull the thread through. Continue working stitches to the end of the row.

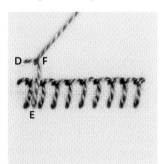

3 | Second row. Emerge at D. Take the thread to the back at E, aligned with the lower edge and between the stitches of the previous row. Emerge through the loop at F.

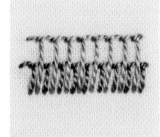

4 | Pull the thread through. Continue working long stitches between the previous to the end of the row.

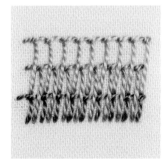

5 | Third row. Work long stitches over the purl edge and between the stitches of the previous row, placing the stitches above the purl edge of the first row.

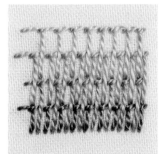

6 | Fourth row. Work long stitches over the purl edge and between the stitches of the previous row.

NEEDLEWEAVING HINTS:

Woven cloth consists of two distinct sets of threads, the warp that runs the length of the cloth and the weft that runs across the cloth. Work a practise piece to ensure that you understand the weaving sequence.

> Work the warp stitches first.

> Leave a gap of approximately one thread width between each stitch.

> Ensure that the warp stitches are taut.

> Always start working the weft at the widest point of the shape. Work down through the sequence of rows eg. 1–8. Return to the starting point. Work up through the sequence of rows eg. 8–1.

> Weft stitches should be straight. If previous rows cause the weaving to bow, your stitches are too close together.

> As the shape narrows, count all weft stitches into the pattern. Even if they are no longer available to work with they still need to be counted or the pattern will be lost.

WOVEN LADDER STITCH

Ladder stitch forms the foundation for weaving in this effective combination, creating a filled band ideal for broad outlines. To work around a curve, place the stitches closer together on the inner edge and further apart on the outer.

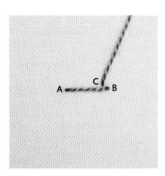

1 | Work a stitch from A to B. Emerge at C, just above the stitch and to the inside of the line.

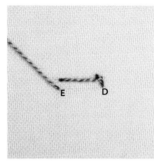

2 | Take the thread to the back at D, below B, and emerge at E, below A.

3 | Slide the needle under the first 'rung' and above the emerging thread at the left-hand side.

4 | Pull the thread through. Slide the needle under both stitches at the right-hand side, above D and below C.

5 | Pull the thread through. Take the thread to the back at F and emerge at G.

6 | Slide the needle under the previous looped thread and the second 'rung' at the left-hand side as shown.

7 | Pull the thread through. Slide the needle under the second 'rung' and the small stitch at the right-hand side.

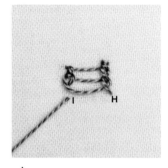

8 | Take the thread to the back on the line below the previous stitches at H and emerge at I.

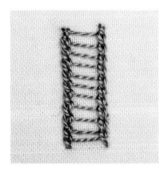

9 | Repeat steps 6–8 to the end of the row. Take the thread to the back at the right-hand side below the last rung.

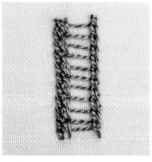

10 | Change thread and emerge at the lower edge. Weave over and under to the top of the row. Take the thread to the back.

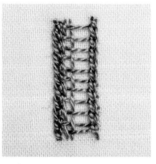

11 | Emerge beside the previous row and weave back to the lower edge. Take the thread to the back.

12 | Continue weaving rows in this manner until the ladder is filled.

WOVEN RAISED CHAIN STITCH

The combination of raised chain stitch with lines of weaving in a contrasting colour creates a unique filling that is delightfully rhythmic to work.

1 | Work a foundation of straight stitches across the shape to be filled.

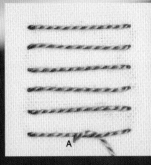

2 | Emerge at A and whip the first stitch: over, under.

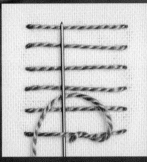

3 | Loop the thread to the left as shown. Take the needle under the first stitch and over the loop.

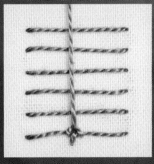

4 | Pull through to complete the first raised chain, forming a knot over the stitch.

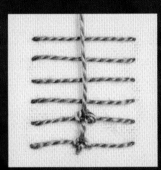

5 | Whip the second stitch and complete the chain in the same manner.

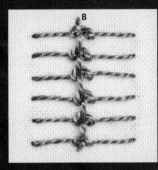

6 | Continue working chains over the foundation stitches to the end of the row. Take the thread to the back at B.

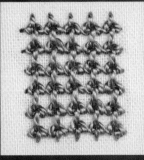

7 | Fill the shape with rows of raised chain in the same manner.

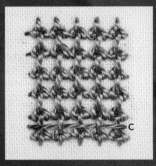

8 | Change thread and emerge at C. Weave over and under between the first two raised chains across the shape. Take the thread to the back at the end of the row.

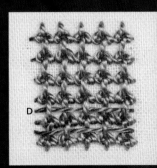

9 | Emerge at D and weave under and over across the shape between the second and third rows of raised chains.

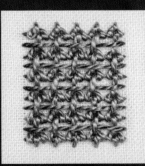

10 | Continue rows of weaving between the raised chains until the shape is filled.

leaping hare

before you begin

We recommend that you read the complete article

See the liftout pattern for the embroidery design and charts

All embroidery is worked with ONE strand of thread

this design uses

Blanket stitch / Blanket stitch bar
Bullion knot
Detached blanket stitch
Double detached blanket stitch bar
Hem stitch
Italian four-sided stitch
Needlewoven picot
Peahole hem stitch
Raised stem stitch
Straight stitch / Twisted cord

The finished sachet measures 29cm x 14.5cm wide (11½" x 5¾").

requirements

FABRIC
38cm (15") square of 32-count antique white linen

SUPPLIES
Contrasting sewing thread
12.5cm (5") embroidery hoop
Sharp embroidery scissors
Erasable fabric marker
Tracing paper
Fine black pen

NEEDLES
No. 24 chenille
No. 4 milliner's
No. 24 tapestry

THREAD
DMC no. 8 perlé cotton
A = 712 cream

preparation for embroidery

PREPARING THE FABRIC
Neaten the edges of the linen with a machine zigzag or overlock stitch to prevent fraying. Working over and under four threads, use the contrasting sewing thread to tack along the vertical centre of the fabric.

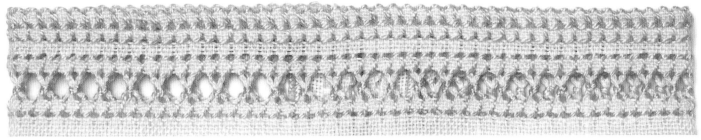

Measure up 4cm (1½") from the lower edge of the fabric along the tacked line and mark with a pin (diag 1).

4cm (1½")

TRANSFERRING THE DESIGN

The hare design is transferred after the border and inner square of the panel have been worked. Trace the design and placement marks onto the tracing paper with the black pen. Using a light box or window, position the design beneath the inner square so that the hare is within the embroidered area and the placement marks are aligned with the straight grain. Using the erasable fabric marker, transfer the body shaping only. Add a dot to mark the lower point of each leg, the upper edge of the head and the tip of each ear.

embroidery

See pages 146–151 for step-by-step instructions for working a double blanket stitch bar, hem stitch variation, Italian four-sided stitch, Italian four-sided stitch filling, needlewoven picot, peahole hem stitch and raised stem stitch.

Refer to the close-up photograph for stitch placement. All embroidery is worked using **A**.

Use the milliner's needle for the bullion knot, the chenille needle for the blanket stitch and the tapestry needle for all other embroidery and construction.

Use the hoop to work the square panel and hare.

ORDER OF WORK

SACHET BORDER

Lower edge

From the marked point on the centre line count 192 fabric threads to the right-hand side and mark. From this point, and working from the right side, embroider Italian four-sided stitch from right to left over 4x4 fabric threads until 96 stitches are complete.

Side and upper edges

Cut and withdraw the next vertical fabric thread to the right and left of the four-sided stitch row.

Rotate the work 90° counter-clockwise so that the four-sided stitch is at the right-hand side. Referring to the step-by-step instructions, embroider hem stitch along the upper edge over 4x4 threads, working from right to left, for 96 stitches. The upper edge of the stitch is worked along the withdrawn thread line.

Cut and withdraw the next vertical fabric thread to the left of the hem stitch. Rotate the work 90° clockwise so that the hem stitch is at the right-hand side. Using the withdrawn thread line as the upper edge of the stitching, embroider hem stitch until reaching the withdrawn thread line at the left-hand side.

Rotate the work 90 degrees clockwise so that the upper band of hem stitch is at the right-hand side. Embroider hem

stitch in the same manner to the four-sided stitch (diag 2).

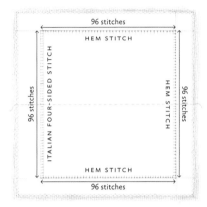

96 stitches

HEM STITCH

ITALIAN FOUR-SIDED STITCH

96 stitches

HEM STITCH

96 stitches

HEM STITCH

HEM STITCH

96 stitches

PANEL

Borders

Referring to the chart, embroider two square borders of Italian four-sided stitch over 4x4 threads on the wrong side of the work.

To begin, count up 40 threads along the centre tacked line from the four-sided stitch at the lower edge and mark with a pin. From this point count 52 threads to the left and embroider four-sided stitch in a square with 26 stitches along each side.

For the inner border, count twelve threads along the centre tacked line from the inner edge of the first border. From this point count 36 threads to the left and work four-sided stitch in a square with 18 stitches per side.

Inner square

Referring to the chart and working from the wrong side, embroider the inner square of 12x12 stitches with four-sided stitch filling.

Border filling

Referring to the chart and working from the right side, embroider pairs of straight stitches to form the crosses. Begin at the top of the border at the right-hand side. Work two pairs of straight stitches, each worked from the inner four-sided stitch border to the centre, to form a triangle.

Continue to embroider triangles in the same manner down the inner border, running the thread behind the four-sided stitches between each triangle. To complete the crosses, work mirror image triangles from the outer border.

Work the crosses around the remaining sides in same manner.

Corners

Referring to the chart, emerge within the second four-sided stitch from the outer corner. Take the thread to the back through the corner square of the inner border. Pick up a single thread and take the thread to the back through the corner square of the outer border. Run the thread behind the border on the next side and emerge through the second stitch from the corner (diag 3).

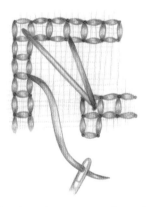

Take the thread once more through the corner square of the inner border and anchor behind the four-sided stitch. Work needleweaving over the spokes to the outer border. Wrap the thread around the nearest spoke, take it to the back and secure.

Repeat for the remaining corners.

Hare

BODY

Referring to page 143, transfer the body shaping to the inner square.

Working from left to right, embroider a framework of blanket stitch over the shape with the purl of the stitches at the lower edge. Place the stitches approximately 3mm (⅛") apart, taking care not to pull them tightly. As you follow the curves, place the stitches closer together on the inner curve and further apart on the outer (diag 4).

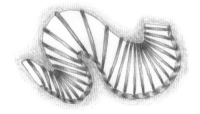

The purl edge of the blanket stitch becomes the first row of the raised stem stitch.

Fill the body with rows of raised stem stitch following the step-by-step instructions. Pack the rows very tightly.

HEAD

The head is a detached blanket stitch triangle. Referring to the close-up photograph, stitch a foundation bar of two straight stitches, each worked from left to right, across the top of the position for the head. Emerge at the left-hand side of the bar and work approximately nine detached blanket stitches over the bar.

Change direction and work detached blanket stitch through the loops of the previous row. There will be one less stitch. Continue working back and forth until one stitch remains, forming a triangular head. Take the thread to the back and secure.

LEGS

Embroider a double blanket stitch bar for each leg following the step-by-step instructions.

EARS

Embroider a needlewoven picot for each ear following the step-by-step instructions.

TAIL

At the position for the tail, use the milliner's needle to work a looped bullion knot.

144

UPPER BAND

A band of peahole hem stitch decorates the upper edge of the sachet.

Preparation

Working from the centre of the upper edge, count down eight fabric threads from the lower edge of the hem stitch. Cut the next thread. Carefully unweave the thread tails back to eight threads from the hem stitch at each side. Fold the tails to the back.

Remove further threads as follows.

Leave 4 / Cut and withdraw 8
Leave 4 / Cut and withdraw 1

On the wrong side, hold the withdrawn thread tails out of the way with a tacking stitch. They will be secured within a blanket stitch edge at each side.

Side edges

Changing to the chenille needle and referring to the chart, work nineteen close blanket stitches at each side of the band of 8 withdrawn threads. Ensure all thread tails are caught under the stitching.

Peahole hem stitch

Working from the wrong side, embroider a row of Italian four-sided stitch over 4x4 threads across the upper band of four fabric threads left between the withdrawn threads. Referring to the step-by-step instructions, work peahole hem stitch across the prepared band. When complete, trim the excess thread tails on the wrong side.

FINISHING AND CONSTRUCTION

BLANKET STITCH BARS

Four pairs of blanket stitch bars hold the twisted cords that close the sachet. See boxes 1–4 in the step-by-step instructions on page 146.

Measure down 5cm (2") from the lower edge of the peahole hem stitch and mark the horizontal fabric thread with a pin. At each side, measure in 4cm (1½") from the inner edge of the hem stitch along the marked fabric thread. Mark these points with a dot using the erasable fabric maker. Working along the same

fabric thread, measure in a further 6cm (2⅜") and mark (diag 5).

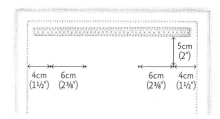

Work two vertical blanket stitch bars down from the marked point. For each bar, work a foundation of two straight stitches over eight fabric threads, ensuring they arch over the fabric so that a cord can pass beneath the completed bar. Cover the foundation with close detached blanket stitch. Ensure the purl edge is to the outside of each bar.

SIDE EDGES

Fold the linen to the back along the outer edge of the hem stitch, ensuring the withdrawn thread line lies on the fold. Working from the right side and sharing holes with the hem stitch, work partial Italian four-sided stitch over the hem stitch. To begin, emerge at **A**, take the thread over the edge at **B** and emerge at C (fig 1).

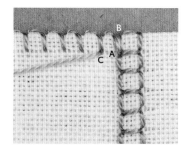

Take the needle from **A** to **C**. Pull the thread through (fig 2).

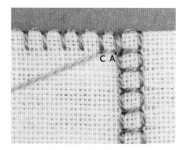

Take the thread over the edge at **D** and emerge at **E** (fig 3).

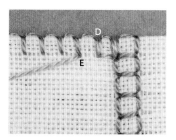

Repeat the sequence along the edge (fig 4).

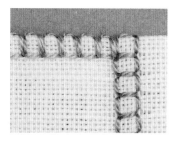

Carefully trim the excess linen close to the stitching. Repeat along the remaining side edge.

UPPER EDGE

Work partial Italian four-sided stitch in a similar manner to the side edges, pulling the thread firmly to draw in the fabric, forming a picot edge. At each corner, work one stitch down the side for reinforcing.

Aligning the stitches, work a second row of Italian four-sided stitch below the upper edge.

CENTRE BACK SEAM

With the wrong side uppermost, bring the two side edges together. Take a stitch through the fabric at the lower edge then begin to whip the seam closed through the outer edge of the hem stitches, whipping twice for each pair of stitches (fig 5).

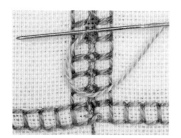

Whip until reaching 8cm (3⅛") below the upper edge and finish off the thread in the hem. Leaving the upper section open will make the sachet easier to use.

LOWER EDGE

Ensuring the four-sided stitches are aligned along the lower edge, adjust the sachet so that the seam becomes the centre back. Whip the lower edge closed through the outer edge of the four-sided stitch. Remove any visible tacking and fabric marker.

TWISTED CORDS

Make two 45cm (18") twisted cords. For each cord, cut eight 1.35m (54") lengths of **A**. Knot the lengths together at each end.

Secure one knotted end over a hook or sewing machine spool pin. Slip a pencil or thin dowel through the second knotted end. Twist the threads until the required tension is achieved. Hold the twisted threads at the centre and bring the ends together. Release the cord from the centre a little at a time until reaching the ends. Knot the ends together and trim away the original knots. Beginning at the left-hand side, thread one cord under the right-hand blanket stitch bar of each pair around the sachet and knot the ends together at the left-hand side. Trim away the previous knot.

Beginning at the right-hand side, thread the remaining cord under the left-hand blanket stitch bars around the sachet and knot the ends together at the right-hand side. Trim away the previous knot. Pull the cords to close the sachet.

DOUBLE BLANKET STITCH BAR
The legs of the hare are created with double blanket stitch bars.

1 | Work a foundation of two straight stitches from A to B.

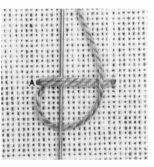

2 | Emerge near A and begin a detached blanket stitch over the foundation.

3 | Pull the thread through.

4 | Work detached blanket stitches to the end of the foundation, keeping them slightly spaced.

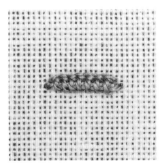

5 | Take the thread to the back beneath the foundation and rotate the work 180°.

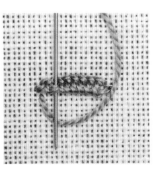

6 | Emerge at the left-hand side and work a detached blanket stitch between the first two stitches.

7 | Work a detached blanket stitch in each space between the previous stitches.

8 | Work the final stitch at the right-hand end and take the thread to the back of the work.

NEEDLEWOVEN PICOT

Picots are ideal for creating petals, sepals and even cute little rabbit or hare ears! This picot is only attached to the fabric at the base. Ensure you have enough thread to finish each picot as it is difficult to join in a new thread.

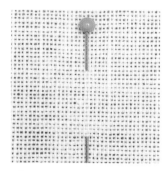

1 | Insert a pin at the position for the picot.

2 | Emerge at A at the position for the left-hand side of the base.

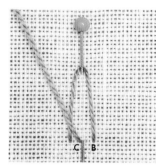

3 | Wrap the thread around the pin, take it to the back at B and emerge at C, the centre-base of the picot.

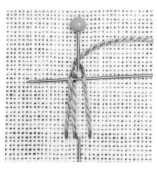

4 | Take the thread around the top of the pin and begin weaving from right to left: under, over, under.

5 | Pull the thread firmly up against the pin. Weave from left to right: over, under, over.

6 | Continue weaving back and forth in this manner, pushing the thread towards the top of the picot as you make each pass.

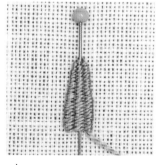

7 | Continue weaving until the foundation threads are completely covered and the weaving is tightly packed.

8 | Take the thread to the back at the base of the picot and secure. Remove the pin.

HEM STITCH

Hem stitch is worked along the side and upper edges. The hem stitch shares holes with the four-sided stitch at the lower corners and with the upper row of hem stitch at the upper corners. Work on the right side of the fabric, from right to left and over four threads. A thread is first withdrawn from the upper edge of the row.

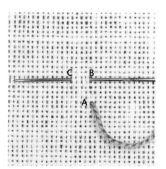

1 | Emerge at A. Take the needle from B to C along the withdrawn thread line.

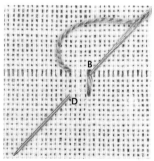

2 | Pull the thread through. Take the needle from B to D.

... HEM STITCH / CONTINUED

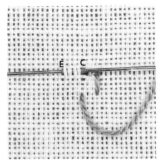  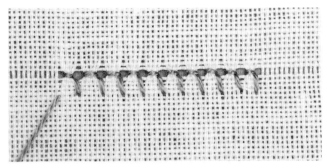

3 | Pull the thread through. Take the needle from C to E.

4 | Pull the thread through. Take the needle from C to F.

5 | Pull the thread through. Continue the sequence to the end of the row.

RAISED STEM STITCH

This stitch is also known as Casalguidi stitch. Usually worked over a foundation of straight stitch, it is worked here over blanket stitch. Take care not to pull the thread too tightly to prevent distortion of the foundation stitches. Use a tapestry needle for the stem stitches which are detached, going over the foundation stitches only.

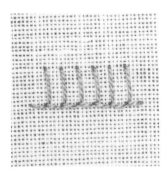 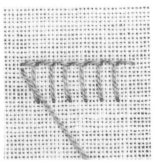 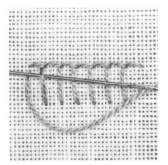 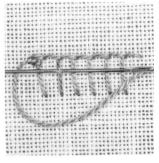

1 | Work the foundation, spacing the stitches 3mm (⅛") apart.

2 | Rotate the work 180°. Emerge at the left-hand side, close to the upper edge.

3 | With the thread looped below, slide the needle from right to left beneath the first foundation stitch.

4 | Pull the thread through. With the thread looped below, slide the needle from right to left beneath the second stitch.

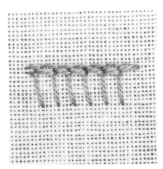  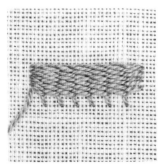 

5 | Continue in the same manner to the end of the row. Take the thread to the back after the last stitch.

6 | Rotate the work 180°. Emerge at the left-hand side and complete the second row in the same manner.

7 | Continue working rows in the same manner, rotating the work 180° after each row and pushing the thread towards the previous row.

8 | Continue until the foundation stitches are completely covered and the rows of raised stem stitch are tightly packed.

ITALIAN FOUR-SIDED STITCH

For the sachet, Italian four-sided stitch is worked along the upper edge of the withdrawn band for the peahole hem stitch. It can be worked from left to right on the wrong side or right to left on the right side of the fabric. Each stitch is over four fabric threads. The stitch is shown here worked from the wrong side.

1 | Take the needle from A to B.

2 | Pull the thread through. Take the needle from C to B.

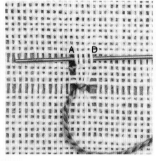

3 | Pull the thread taut. Take the needle from D to A.

4 | Pull the thread taut. Take the needle form D to C.

5 | Pull the thread taut. Take the needle from E to C.

6 | Pull the thread taut. Continue working the row, following steps 3-5.

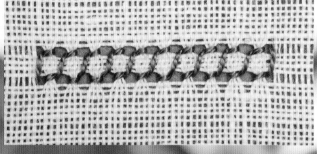

7 | Right side of work.

PEAHOLE HEM STITCH

Work this decorative hem stitch from left to right on the wrong side of the work. First work a row of Italian four-sided stitch along the upper edge of the withdrawn thread band. The peahole hem stitch is incorporated into four-sided stitch along the lower edge.

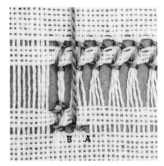

1 | Complete one Italian four-sided stitch and begin the next, taking the thread from A to B.

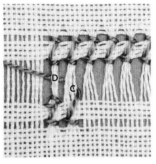

2 | Take the thread from C to D, picking up two thread bundles.

3 | Take the needle behind the bundles again, with the thread under the needle tip.

4 | Pull the thread through firmly, forming a knot at the centre of the bundles.

5 | Take the needle behind the bundles again, with the thread under the needle tip.

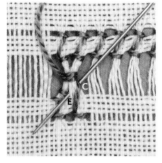

6 | Pull taut. Take the needle behind the bundles at C and emerge between them at E.

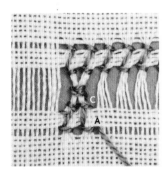

7 | Take the thread from C to A to complete the second four-sided stitch.

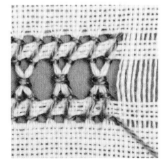

8 | Repeat the stitch sequence from 1–7 across the row.

9 | Right side of work.

ITALIAN FOUR-SIDED STITCH FILLING

This stitch creates the background stitching for Casalguidi embroidery.
Rows of Italian four-sided stitch are worked from the wrong side of the fabric. After the first row, partial stitches are worked to ensure that the adjoining edges on the right side of the work each have only one stitch. On the wrong side, all diagonal stitches should be worked in the same direction.

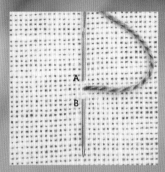

1 | Row 1. Take the needle to the back at A and emerge at B.

2 | Take the needle to the back at C and re-emerge at B.

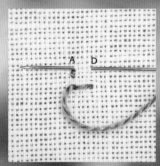

3 | Take the needle to the back at D and emerge at A.

4 | Repeat steps 1-3 to the end of the row.

5 | Row 2, above. Rotate the work 180°. Work in a similar manner to row 1, omitting the lower stitch in step 2.

6 | Row 3, below. Rotate the work 180°. Work in a similar manner to row 1, omitting the upper stitch in step 3.

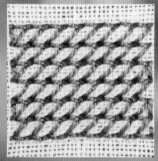

7 | Continue working rows above and below in the same manner as rows 2 and 3 for the required number of rows.

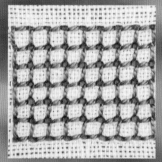

8 | Right side of the work.

edinburgh etui

before you begin

We recommend that you read the complete article and instructions in the liftout pattern

See the liftout pattern for the templates and alphabet

All embroidery is worked with ONE strand of thread unless specified

this design uses

Back stitch / Beading
Cross stitch / Eyelet variation
Four-sided stitch / French knots
Hedebo stitch loop
Long and short blanket stitch
Long and short stitch
Long-arm cross stitch
Rhodes stitch / Satin stitch
Smyrna cross stitch
Spiral trellis stitch / Straight stitch
Tent stitch / Trellis couching

The finished etui measures
15cm x 10cm wide (6" x 4").

requirements

FABRIC

35.5cm x 61cm wide (14" x 24") piece of platinum 32-count linen

35cm x 75cm wide (14" x 30") piece of sea green silk dupion

15cm x 30cm wide (6" x 12") piece of royal purple silk dupion

13cm x 18cm wide (5" x 7") piece of ivory cotton broadcloth

SUPPLIES

18cm x 25cm wide (7⅛" x 10") piece of lightweight fusible interfacing

13cm x 30cm wide (5" x 12") piece of heavyweight fusible interfacing

23cm x 46cm wide (9" x 18") piece of heavyweight interlining

23cm x 33cm wide (9" x 12") piece of Mylar® (polyester film)

Slate or scroll frame to fit fabric

Strong thread (lacing)

5cm x 7.5cm wide (2" x 3") piece of gold wool felt

Ivory sewing thread

Purple sewing thread

Contrasting sewing thread

Green beading thread to match silk

Adhesive tape

Craft knife

Long ruler

Dressmaker's awl

Small amount of fibre-fill

6cm x 8cm wide (2⅜" x 3⅛") piece of firm card

6mm oval green crystal bead (1)

4mm square amber crystal bead (1)

4mm oval purple crystal bead (1)

3cm x 2cm wide (1¼" x ¾")
Sylvan Treasures wooden thistle

Silver thistle charm (optional)

Tracing paper

Fine black pen

Fine heat-soluble fabric marker

NEEDLES

No. 10 milliner's
No. 24 tapestry
No. 26 tapestry

THREADS & BEADS

DMC no. 12 perlé cotton
A = 524 vy lt fern green

Gloriana silk chenille
B = 000 soft white (20cm)

Gloriana stranded silk thread
C = 89 twilight
D = 96 summer foliage
E = 102 fresh snow
F = 141 sandstone rose
G = 150 sage
H = 151 cinnamon
I = 153 olallieberry
J = 160 Blythe green
K = 169 old gold
L = 201 hazelnut
M = 206 olivine
N = 211 antique black
O = 213 thistle patch

Miyuki no. 8 seed beads
P = 157 transparent amethyst (145)

Miyuki Delica no. 15 seed beads
Q = 0100 transparent lt topaz (100)

preparation for embroidery

PREPARING THE FABRIC

Neaten the raw edges of the linen with a machine zigzag or overlock stitch to prevent fraying.

TRANSFERRING THE DESIGN

Work all tacking lines along the grain-lines using the contrasting sewing thread.

At the upper left-hand corner of the linen rectangle measure in and mark 5cm (2") from the upper and side edges.

Beginning at this point and working over and under four threads, mark out each piece following the diagram and pin cushion graph (diag 1).

> **NOTE:** On the upper and lower edges of the pin cushion there is a compensating stitch worked over two threads. Work under or over only two threads at this point.

Mount the fabric on the frame with the etui side panels fully visible. Once the side panels, pin cushion and scissor

fob panels have been worked adjust the fabric in the frame if necessary so that the remaining pieces can be stitched.

Using the black pen trace the rose, thistle and shamrock templates onto the tracing paper twice. You should have two roses, six thistles and six shamrocks.

Using a lightbox or window if necessary, trace the templates onto the ivory broad-cloth using the heat-soluble marker.

embroidery

See pages 162–163 for step-by-step instructions for working the Hedebo stitch loop, Rhodes stitch and spiral trellis stitch.

Refer to the close-up photograph and charts for colour placement.

Use the milliner's needle for all surface embroidery, the no. 24 tapestry needle for the cotton perlé and two strands of silk, and the no. 26 tapestry for one strand of silk.

> **CHARTS:** The representation of the lines and squares on the charts varies. Refer to the instructions for each individual piece for the correct information.

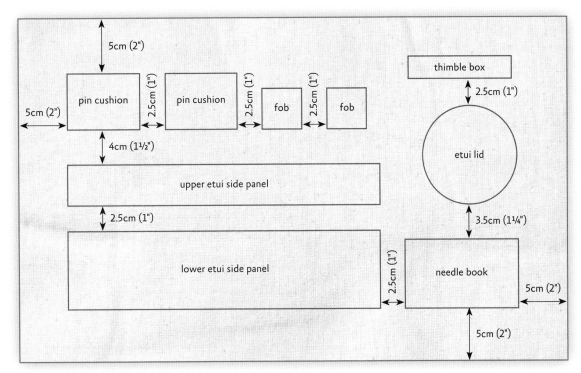

Diag 1

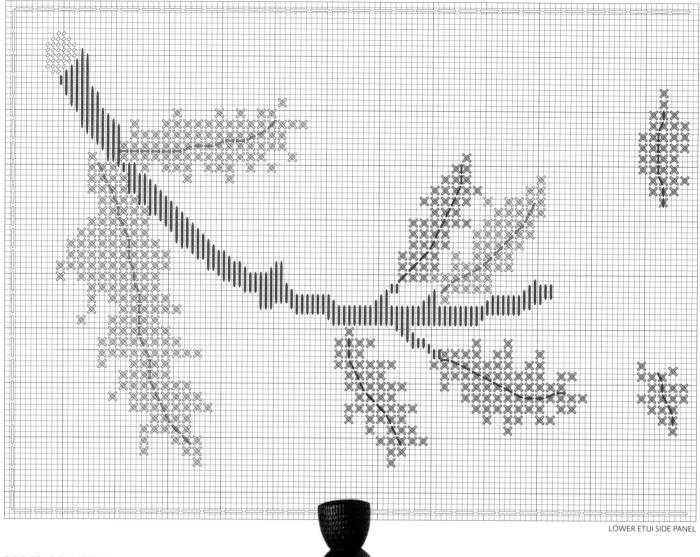

LOWER ETUI SIDE PANEL

ORDER OF WORK

HINT: When working cross stitch with variegated threads complete each cross before moving onto the next.

LOWER ETUI SIDE PANEL

CHART: Each line on the graph represents a fabric thread.

Using **A** stitch the outer border of the panel with back stitch over four threads removing the tacking as you work. Carefully count the back stitches on the upper and lower edges and mark the centre. You should have ninety-six stitches on each edge and the centre will fall between the forty-eighth and forty-ninth stitches. Work a line of tacking down the fabric at this point using the contrasting sewing

thread to mark the centre.

Stem

Work the main stems in satin stitch using two strands of **L**. Stitch the small area at the base of each stem with tent stitch over 1 x 1 threads using **K**.

Leaves

Embroider the leaves with cross stitch using **D** and **J**. Once the leaves are complete stitch the veins in back stitch using **L** and **M** and working over the cross stitches where necessary.

Rose

Cut one rose template from the broadcloth. Using the photograph as a guide, position the broadcloth shape on the linen between the leaves and stitch in place with small straight stitches perpendicular to the edge using **F**.

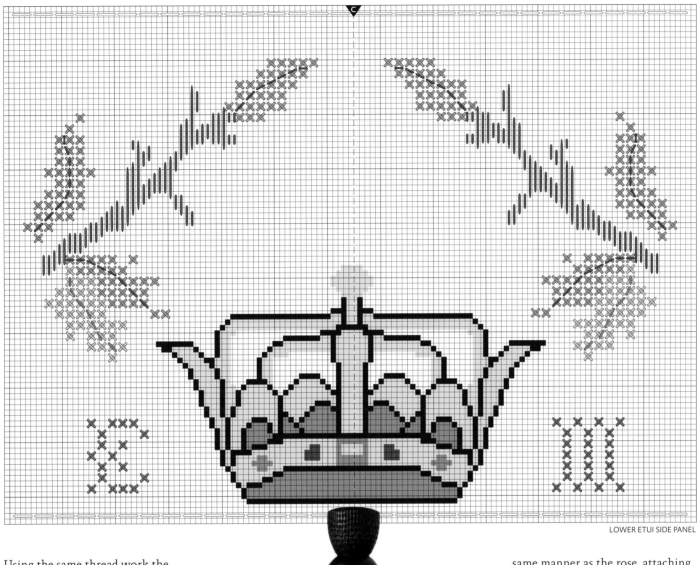

LOWER ETUI SIDE PANEL

Using the same thread work the outer edge of each petal with long and short blanket stitch, working the long stitches halfway down the petal. Leaving an unstitched area adjacent to the centre and along each edge, fill the remainder of the petal with long and short stitch using **E**. Work the remaining area with **H** bringing some long stitches up into the blanket stitch and taking care to ensure that there are long stitches along the edge of the petal. These stitches help define each petal. Fill the centre of the flower with French knots using two strands of **K**.

Repeat for the second rose on the remaining half of the design.

Thistle

Cut one set of three thistle templates from the broadcloth. Stitch each template in place in the

same manner as the rose, attaching the two large thistles close to the base of the stem and the small thistle near the tip.

Cover the base of each thistle with satin stitch using **J** and working down the shape. Begin stitching at the centre and work across to one edge before returning to the centre and completing the remainder of the shape.

Fill the upper area with satin stitch using **C** making every third stitch slightly longer. Begin stitching at the centre with a long stitch and finish just over the broadcloth on each edge with a long stitch. Work spaced straight stiches from the base of the upper area using **I**.

Using **D** for the long straight stitches and small couching stitches, work trellis couching over the base of each thistle.

155

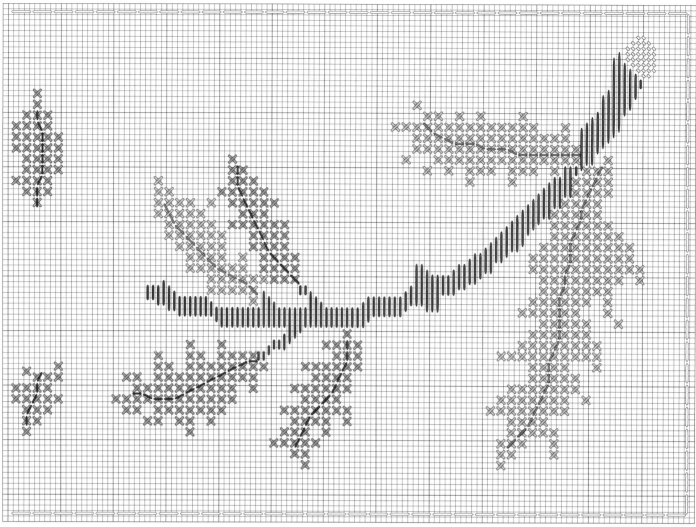

LOWER ETUI SIDE PANEL

Repeat for the second set of thistles on the remaining half of the design.

Shamrock

Cut one set of three shamrock templates from the broadcloth. Stitch each template in place in the same manner as the rose.

Each shamrock is made up of three small heart shapes and each one is individually filled with satin stitch. Using **M** begin stitching a heart by working a stitch down the centre from the upper indentation to the point. Fill one side of the heart then return to the centre and stitch the remaining side. Complete the two remaining hearts on each shamrock in the same manner.

Repeat for the second set of shamrocks on the remaining half of the design.

Crown

Using the line of tacking as a guide, centre the crown and work in tent stitch using **G**, **H**, **K** and **N** over 1 x 1 threads. The lower edge of the crown should be two threads above the back stitch border.

Initials

Choose the desired initials from the alphabet and work in cross stitch using **H**. Betsy's initials are shown only for placement purposes. The lower edge of each letter should be four threads above the back stitch line and they should be evenly spaced on each side of the crown.

UPPER ETUI SIDE PANEL

CHART: Each line on the graph represents a fabric thread.

Using **A** stitch the outer border of the panel with back stitch over four threads removing the tacking as you work. Carefully count the back stitches on the upper and lower edges and mark the centre. You should have ninety-six stitches on each edge and the centre will fall between the forty-eighth and forty-ninth stitches. Work a line of tacking down the fabric at this point using the contrasting sewing thread to mark the centre.

Upper border

Work the border in back stitch using **O** and beginning at the tacked centre line. Stitch the tassel cords in the same manner beginning four threads below the point of each picot.

Swag

Stitch the swag with satin stitch using two strands of **K** and beginning at the tacked centre line.

Tassels

Using **H**, work each tassel head with spiral trellis stitch or an octagonal Rhodes stitch if preferred. Work the skirt with satin stitch using two strands of **G**.

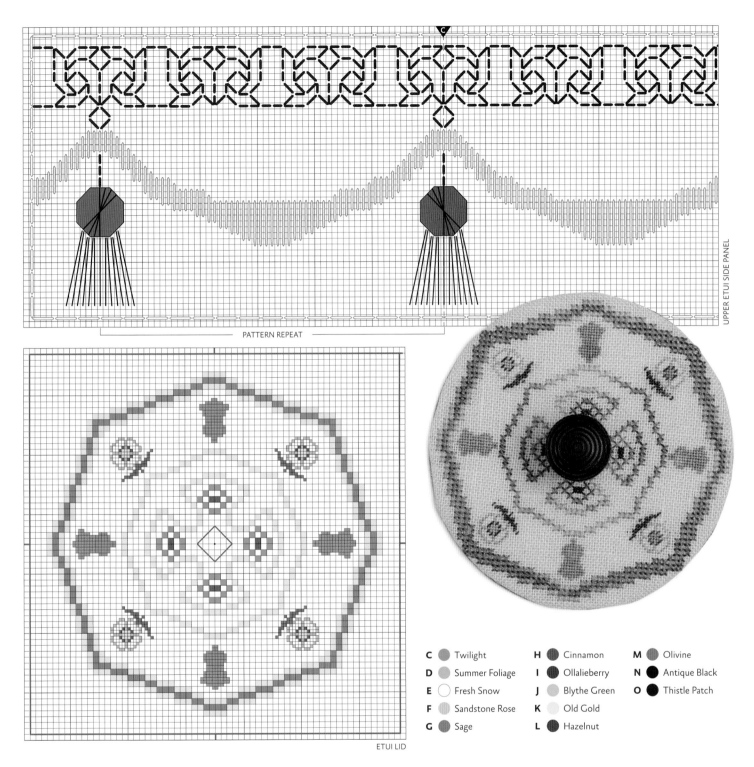

PATTERN REPEAT

C	⬤ Twilight	**H**	⬤ Cinnamon	**M**	⬤ Olivine
D	⬤ Summer Foliage	**I**	⬤ Ollalieberry	**N**	⬤ Antique Black
E	◯ Fresh Snow	**J**	⬤ Blythe Green	**O**	⬤ Thistle Patch
F	⬤ Sandstone Rose	**K**	⬤ Old Gold		
G	⬤ Sage	**L**	⬤ Hazelnut		

ETUI LID

ETUI LID

CHART: Each square on the graph represents 2 x 2 fabric threads.

The outer band, inner line and quatrefoil motif are worked over 2 x 2 threads. The rose and thistle motifs are worked over 1 x 1 threads.

The lid does not have a back stitch border.

Stitch the outer band in cross stitch using **G** for the centre and **K** for the outer lines. Work the inner line in the same manner using **K**. Stitch the quatrefoil with cross stitch using **K** for the outer edge and **D** and **H** for the inner motifs.

Embroider the thistles with tent stitch using **D** for the base and **C** for the upper section. Work the roses in the same manner using **F** for the petal outlines,

E and **H** for the petals, **K** for the centre and **M** for the leaves.

Using **A** stitch an eyelet at the lid centre using the graph as a guide to stitch placement. Open the centre with the awl before stitching the eyelet. As you work the eyelet keep firm tension on the thread to keep the hole open. The hole must be large enough for the base of the wooden thistle to be inserted.

157

PINCUSHION

CHART: Each square on the graph represents 2 x 2 fabric threads.

Using **A** stitch the outer border of each panel with back stitch over four threads taking care to work the compensating stitch at the upper and lower edges over two threads. Remove the tacking as you work.

Front

Work the tartan pattern with cross stitch using **F**, **I**, **J**, **K** and **N**.

Back

Stitch the central design with cross stitch using **F**, **G**, **J** and **N**.

If desired, work the year in cross stitch using **I**, placing a number in each corner as shown.

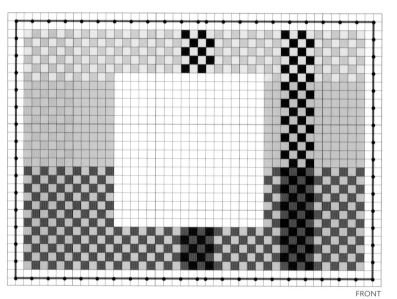

FRONT

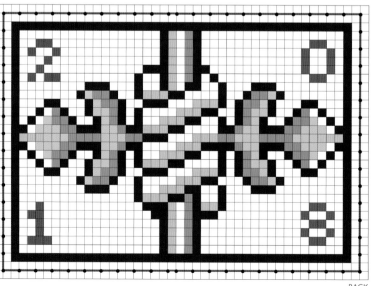

BACK

SCISSOR FOB

CHART: Each line on the graph represents a fabric thread.

Using **A** stitch the outer border of each panel with back stitch over four threads removing the tacking as you work.

Front

Work the three diamonds that run through the centre of the design in Rhodes stitch using **E**. Stitch the zigzag band on each side of the centre with straight stitch using **D** for the upper and **H** for the lower lines. Work a line of diamond eyelets using **I** for the upper section and **G** for the lower. Fill the remaining areas with four-sided

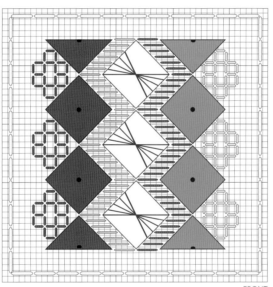

FRONT

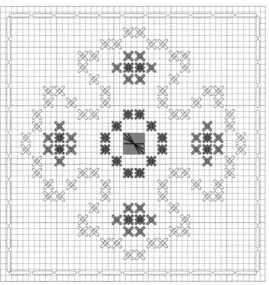

BACK

stitch using **L** for the upper and **K** for the lower sections.

Back

Stitch the quatrefoil in cross stitch using **H**, **K** and **M**. Work a Rhodes stitch at the centre using **M**.

THIMBLE HOLDER

CHART: Each line on the graph represents a fabric thread.

Using **A** stitch the outer border of the panel with back stitch over four threads removing the tacking as you work.

Stitch the outer borders with long-arm cross stitch using **K**. Work the spaced Smyrna cross stitch using **I** and the angled satin stitch bands using **K** taking care to ensure that

159

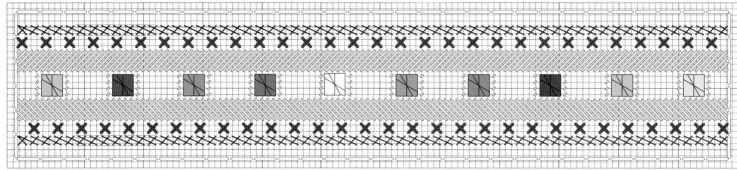

the stitches in each band are worked in opposing directions. Using the colours indicated stitch the jewels along the centre of the band with Rhodes stitch. Work a tent stitch border down each side of each one over 1 x 1 fabric threads using **K**. On one long edge and using the ivory sewing thread, couch the length of **B** in place just below the border of long-arm cross stitch. Leaving 1cm (⅜") extending past the stitching on each end, trim away the excess thread. This will be the lower edge of the crown.

NEEDLEBOOK

CHART: Each line on the graph represents a fabric thread.

Using **A** stitch the outer border and dividing lines of the panel, following the shaping on the graph, with back stitch over four threads removing the tacking as you work.

Stitch the leaves on each section with cross stitch using **D**, **J** and **M** and the stems with **M**. Work the flower petals with Smyrna cross stitch using **K** and the centres with square or octagonal Rhodes stitch using **H**. Embroider two eyelets on the purse flap using the same thread.

Choose letters from the alphabet and work on the centre section in cross stitch using **H**.

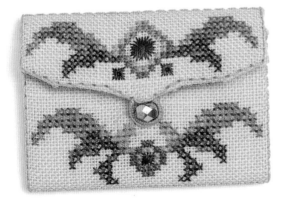

construction

See the liftout pattern.

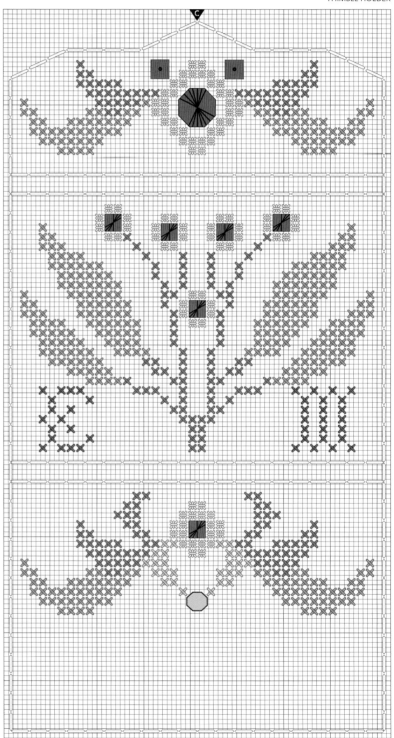

RHODES STITCH

Rhodes stitch is created with straight stitch spokes moving in a twist around the shape, creating a subtle touch of dimension in a block of colour. For the neatest appearance, the first stitch should be just before one of the points so that the final stitch is point-to-point.

1 | Work a stitch across the shape.

2 | Work a second stitch across the first.

3 | Continue working stitches, moving in the same direction around the shape.

4 | The stitch is complete when every fabric hole around the edge of the shape has been used once.

HEDEBO STITCH LOOP

A Hedebo stitch loop is used to close the needlebook and thimble holder. The height of the loop is determined by the tension of the initial cross stitch. The looser the threads, the more height the loop will have.

1 | For the base of the loop, work a long cross stitch. Re-emerge at the left-hand side.

2 | **Hedebo stitch.** Take the thread under the cross stitch from top to bottom, leaving a small loop.

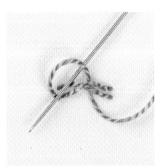

3 | Take the needle through the loop, from back to front.

4 | Pull the thread through to tighten the knot, pulling the stitch to the left-hand end of the base threads.

5 | Repeat steps 2–4 to cover the base threads with Hedebo stitch. Ensure each stitch is pulled snugly against the previous to fill the loop.

6 | To finish, take the thread to the back at the right-hand side and secure.

SPIRAL TRELLIS STITCH

The knotted texture and slight dome of this stitch is ideal for the tassel heads around the upper side panel of the etui. To create a higher dome, work more rounds of the spiral trellis before decreasing. To create a flatter dome, work fewer rounds before decreasing. The stitch can be worked in either a clockwise or counter-clockwise direction; work in the same manner for each tassel head so that the spiral is consistent around the etui. The back stitch framework for the spiral trellis can be any shape; here it is octagonal.

1 | Framework. Outline the shape with back stitch over two threads. Emerge between the first and last stitches.

2 | Round 1. With the tip pointing outwards, slide the needle under the first stitch. Wrap the thread over and under the needle tip.

3 | Holding the wrap in place, pull the thread through to form a knot.

4 | Repeat steps 2–3 for each back stitch around the shape.

5 | Round 2. Slide the needle beneath the thread from round 1, just before the first knot. Wrap the needle tip as before.

6 | Pull the thread through.

7 | Work a stitch on the thread bar between each knot around the shape, continuing until the desired height is reached.

8 | Decrease. Work in a similar manner to step 7, skipping every second or third stitch until reaching the centre.

9 | Take the needle to the back over a thread bar across from the last stitch.

10 | Completed spiral trellis stitch.

the linnet

before you begin

We recommend that you read the complete article

See the liftout pattern for the embroidery design and wing template

All embroidery is worked with ONE strand of thread unless specified

this design uses

Appliqué / Back stitch / Beading
Chipping / Couching
French knot / Long and short stitch
Purls over string padding
Satin stitch / Split stitch
Stem stitch / Straight stitch

The finished design measures
20cm x 16cm wide (8" x 6¼").

requirements

FABRIC

40cm (16") square of pale blue silk dupion

40cm (16") square of medium weight calico (muslin)

10cm (4") square of gold lurex

SUPPLIES

10cm (4") square of fusible webbing

Pale blue sewing thread

30cm (12") embroidery hoop with the inner ring bound

Clear beading thread

Beeswax

Velvet cutting pad

Goldwork scissors

Blunt-nose tweezers

Mellor

Tracing paper

Fine black pen

Fine heat-soluble fabric marker

NEEDLES

No. 18 chenille
No. 9 crewel
No. 10 crewel
No. 12 sharp

THREADS, SEQUINS & BEADS

Au ver à Soie, soie d'Alger
stranded silk
A = 1341 vy lt blue-violet
B = 1342 lt blue-violet
C = 1343 blue-violet
D = 2121 ultra lt parrot green
E = 2133 hunter green
F = 2136 vy dk hunter green
G = 3021 vy lt burgundy
H = 3023 burgundy

I = 3026 vy dk burgundy
J = 3433 sable
K = 3441 vy lt steel grey
L = 3442 lt steel grey
M = 3444 med steel grey
N = 4096 optical white
O = 4106 black

Au ver à Soie, metallic tressé 16
metallic thread
P = 005 black

Au ver à Soie, metallic un fil
metallic thread
Q = 019 black/silver
R = 001 silver

DMC **soft cotton**
S = 2101 copper
T = 2310 black
U = 2415 pearl grey

DMC Diamant **metallic thread**
V = 3852 gold

Gütermann **sewing thread**
W = 000 black
X = 8 lt grey
Y = 488 gold

Z = 497 steel grey
AA = 800 white
AB = 842 tan

YLI #100 silk thread
AC = 229 yellow

Metal threads
AD = ivory millary–15cm (6")
AE = no. 12 (K2) silver Japanese thread–35cm (14")
AF = fine gilt rococo–90cm (36")
AG = medium gilt rococo–1.8m (1yd 35")
AH = no. 6 gilt passing–30cm (12")
AI = no. 8 copper bright check purl–10cm (4")
AJ = no. 8 gilt bright check purl–15cm (6")
AK = no. 8 silver bright check purl–45cm (18")
AL = no. 8 copper smooth purl–15cm (6")
AM = no. 8 black wire check purl–30cm (12")
AN = no. 8 copper wire check purl–10cm (4")
AO = copper super pearl purl–5cm (2")

PAILLETTES & SEQUINS

AP = 2mm gold paillettes (40)
AQ = 3mm *Annie Penin* silver-mauve cupped sequin CV 2005 (18)
AR = 3mm matte silver sequin (5)
AS = 4mm black sequin (1)
AT = 4mm cupped gold sequin (3)
AU = 4mm *Swarovski* cornflower crystal sequin (1)
AV = 5mm *Swarovski* gold crystal sequin (1)

BEADS

AW = 3mm silver bicone crystal (2)

Miyuki no. 11 seed beads
AX = 522 aqua Ceylon (5)
AY = 42 silver-lined gold (35)

Miyuki no. 15 seed beads
AZ = 42 silver-lined gold (7)

Miyuki 3mm bugle beads
BA = 020 dk sapphire (2)

2mm 2-cut bugle beads
BB = gold (11)

preparation for embroidery

PREPARING THE FABRICS

Neaten the raw edges of the silk and calico with a machine zigzag or overlock stitch to prevent fraying.

TRANSFERRING THE DESIGN

Using the black pen trace the embroidery design and placement marks onto the tracing paper. Tape the tracing to a lightbox or window. Centre the silk over the tracing aligning the placement marks with the straight grain of the fabric and tape in place. Using the heat-soluble marker trace the bird and flower design. Mark in the placement for the cage with small dots spaced 1cm (³⁄₈") apart on the straight lines and 5mm (³⁄₁₆") apart on the curves.

Aligning the edges, place the calico behind the silk and mount both fabrics in the hoop ensuring they are taut. Using the pale blue sewing thread in the no.10 crewel needle, make tiny stab stitches through both layers along all the main design lines at 1cm (³⁄₈") intervals.

Centre the piece of fusible webbing, paper side uppermost, over the wing template and trace the shaping using the black pen. Fuse the webbing to the wrong side of the gold lurex.

embroidery

See pages 169 and 171 for step-by-step instructions for working the string padding and purls over string padding.

Refer to the close-up photograph for colour placement.

Use the no. 9 crewel needle for all silk embroidery, the no. 10 crewel for attaching the beads and sequins, the no. 12 sharp for attaching the cut metal threads and the chenille needle to sink the metal thread tails.

All embroidery is worked in the hoop.

SILK EMBROIDERY

Legs

Using **J**, outline the legs and feet with split stitch and fill with satin stitch, working over the outline. Changing to **M**, embroider each claw with satin stitch.

Beak

Outline the beak with split stitch using **L**. Fill with satin stitch using **M** and **O** for the lower half and **L** and **O** for the upper.

Eye

Outline the eye with three rows of split stitch using **M** for the outer row, **L** for the centre row and **K** for the inner row. Fill the centre of the shape with satin stitch using **N**. Using the photograph as a guide to placement, attach the **AS** sequin with a two-wrap French knot using **N**. Once the remaining head embroidery is complete, outline the eye with back stitch using **R**.

Head

Fill the head with long and short stitch radiating the stitches out from the eye and using **K**, **L**, **M** and **N**. Add several straight stitches above the eye with **H** and under the eye, along the back of the head and through the white stitches just above the rose with **Q**.

Upper breast

Fill the upper breast with long and short stitch using **L** and **M**.

Rose

Outline each rose petal with split stitch using **G** or **H**. Using the photograph as a guide, fill the petals with long and short stitch using **G**, **H** and **I**, covering the split stitch outlines. Once all other

165

embroidery is complete, stitch an arch of seven paillettes (**AP**) around the centre using a waxed length of **AC**. Stitch a crystal sequin (**AV**) in the centre of the flower using the same thread.

Belly

Work the stems in stem stitch and the leaves in satin stitch using **N**. Attach an **AR** sequin at the centre of each flower with an **AX** bead and the beading thread. Using **N**, work French knots around the edge of each sequin as indicated in the photograph. Alternating between **N** and **Q**, work radiating straight stitches around each sequin to create flower petals. Work back stitch around each leaf and along one side of each stem with **Q**.

Tail feather

Outline the tail feather with split stitch using **M** for the upper half and **O** for the lower. Cover each half of the feather with satin stitch using **M** and **O** for the upper half and **O** for the lower. Add 2–3 straight stitches over the lower half using **R** and work the centre line in back stitch using the same thread.

Flax flowers

Outline the three large petals with split stitch using **B**. Fill the petals with long and short stitch beginning with **C** at the base and changing to **B** at the upper edge. Work straight stitches over the petals as indicated using **A**. Work the thin curved petal with satin stitch using **A**. Stitch the lower section of the flower in long and short stitch beginning with **E** at the base and shading through **A** to **B** below the light petal. Embroider the buds in long and short stitch beginning at the base with **E** and changing to **D**. Work the stems, leaves and sepals in stem stitch using **F**.

METAL THREAD EMBROIDERY

> **NOTE:** Wax each length of the yellow silk thread, **AC**, before use. Use the velvet pad and goldwork scissors when cutting the metal threads.

Gold wing

Cut out the wing from the webbing backed lurex and discard the paper. Aligning the edges of the fabric with the design lines, position the wing, webbing side down, and carefully fuse in place. On the design tracing use a large needle to pierce a hole through the paper at the centre of each wing flower and the upper and lower ends of the dividing lines. Position the tracing over the lurex shape and, using the heat-soluble marker, transfer the markings to the lurex. Using **Y**, work a long straight stitch between the upper and lower markings of each dividing line. These two stitches are removed once the metal thread lines have been stitched in place. At the centre of each large flower attach an **AT** sequin with an **AY** bead using **AC**. Surround each sequin with eight paillettes (**AP**) stitched in place with **AC**. The pailletes should just fit between the thread lines. At the centre of each small flower attach a paillette (**AP**) with **AC**. Using the same thread attach a circle of six **AY** beads around each complete flower and five **AY** beads around the incomplete flower on the lower left-hand edge.

Add two **BB** leaves beneath each complete small flower and one beneath the incomplete flower using **AC**. Add a pair of leaves in the same manner at the top of the left-hand section.

After the long back feathers have been worked, outline and divide the wing sections in the following manner. Leaving a 1cm (³⁄₈") tail at each end, couch a length of **AF** around the wing shape using **AC**. Couch a line down each division in the same manner. Sink the thread tails and secure to the calico on the back of the work. Remove the thread division lines.

Long back feathers

There are six black and silver stripes that form the back feathers. Leave 1cm (³⁄₈") tails at each end of each length of thread.

STRIPE 1 – Beginning beneath the tip of the gold wing couch a doubled length of **AE** in place with a waxed length of **AA**, staggering the length at the ends. Using the photograph as a guide, add couching stitches using **Z** as indicated.

STRIPE 2 – Beginning beneath the tip of the gold wing couch a length of **P** in place with a waxed length of **W**. Couch two more lengths of **P** in place beginning beneath the gold feather and tapering the tip.

STRIPE 3 – Beginning beneath the gold feather, couch a doubled length of **AE** in place with a waxed length of **AA**, staggering the length at the ends.

STRIPE 4 – Couch a doubled length of **P** in place with a waxed length of **W**.

STRIPE 5 – Couch a single length of **AE** in place with a waxed length of **AA**.

STRIPE 6 – Couch a doubled length of **P** in place with a length of **R**, adding additional stitches as indicated.

Finishing

Sink the thread tails and secure to the calico on the back of the work.

Gold feather

Leaving 1cm (³⁄₈") tails at each end, couch pairs of lengths of **AH** in place with **AC**, offsetting the couching stitches in each row. Sink the thread tails and secure to the calico on the back of the work.

Copper feather

Cut a 25cm (10") length of **S**. Wax the length then run between your fingers to remove any excess wax. From

Sequin feather

Using the photograph as a guide to placement, stitch the **AQ** sequins in place with a waxed length of **Z**, beginning at the top of the shape and overlapping each one.

Tail feather

Working in the same manner as the copper feather, pad the lower half using five, 7cm (2¾") waxed strands of **T** and a doubled, waxed length of **W** and the upper half with five, 7cm (2¾") waxed strands of **U** and a doubled, waxed length of **X**. Cover each half of the feather with **AK** and **AM**. Stitch the black purls in place with a waxed length of **W** and the silver purls with a waxed length of **X**.

Belly

Using **V**, couch the length of **AD** along the underside of the belly, trimming the ends to fit neatly along the line.

Crown

Beginning at the back of the head and leaving a 1cm (⅜") tail at each end, couch a length of **AH** along the marked lines using **AC**. Sink the tails and secure to the calico on the back of the work. Along the base of the crown attach the **AU** sequin at the centre, a **BA** bugle bead at each end and the **AW** crystals in between using the beading thread. Stitch the markings in straight stitch using **V**, working a cross stitch overlapped with a vertical straight stitch (diag 1).

the length cut four, 5cm (2") lengths. Centre the waxed lengths over one side of the feather and, commencing at the centre, begin couching the threads in place with a waxed, double length of **AB**, working the stitches 2mm (¹⁄₁₆") apart. Taper the padding at each end of the shape by trimming away the two lower padding threads 6mm (¼") from the end of the shape. Continue couching the remaining padding threads until 3mm (⅛") from the ends and trim away the remaining padding threads at an angle just inside the marked line. Couch the tails firmly into place. Repeat for the second side of the feather taking care to ensure that the centre line remains uncovered. The padding is covered with cut lengths of **AI**, **AL** and **AN** that are attached in the same way as beads with a waxed length of **AB**. Begin covering the lower

half of the feather at the widest point of the shape. Bring the thread to the front on the outer edge of the padding. Thread on a length of purl and take the needle to the back close to the centre line taking care to ensure that the purl sits at a 45° angle. Continue adding lengths of purl, taking care to maintain the angle. Reduce the length of the purls as necessary to fill the shape. Work the upper side of the feather in the same manner.

Using a waxed length of **AB**, couch a length of **AO** down the centre of the feather.

Chipped background

Cut sufficient 1mm (¹⁄₃₂") lengths of **AJ** and **AK** to cover the area. Stitch the chips in place with a doubled length of **AC** taking care to ensure that the adjacent chips face in different directions.

Fill the narrow band above the base with 1mm (¹⁄₃₂") chips of **AK** attached with **AA**.

In each lobe of the centre trefoil, at the base of the end trefoils and the tip of the single lobes, stitch an **AZ** bead with **AC**.

Attach a 1mm (¹⁄₃₂") chip of **AK** using **AA** in each lobe of the end trefoils and beneath the upper shaped line.

Cage

Leave 1cm (³⁄₈") tails at each end of each length of metal thread.

Beginning at the lower right-hand corner, couch **AG** around the outer edge of the cage using **AC**. Work two more arched lines in the same manner to complete the vertical bars. Couch the loop at the top of the cage in the same manner.

Using **AF** couch the horizontal bars in place with **AC** as indicated in the photograph, stopping and starting threads at all intersections. Work the small areas between the toes with straight stitch using **V**. Sink all thread tails and secure to the calico on the back of the work.

STRING PADDING

This type of padding is often used under narrow, tapered shapes and covered with cut purls. The soft cotton thread is waxed to ensure it is firm and pliable before it is couched in place using waxed matching sewing thread. We used contrasting threads for clarity.

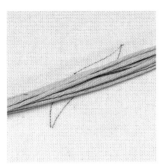

1 | Cut and wax the required number of cotton threads and place together in a bundle. Position the bundle along the shape ensuring the threads are straight and parallel.

2 | Bring the thread to the front at the widest point, just inside the design line. Take the needle to the back just inside the design line on the opposite side of the cotton padding.

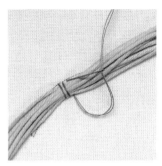

3 | Continue working stitches over the padding threads 2mm (¹⁄₁₆") apart in the same manner, pulling the padding threads firmly together.

4 | As the shape begins to taper, lift the upper cotton threads and trim a few threads from underneath as close as possible to the couching.

5 | Continue to couch the bundle in place, gradually trimming the cotton threads as you near the tip.

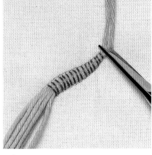

6 | At the tip, trim any remaining underlying threads just back from the design line. Trim the upper threads on the design line.

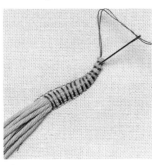

7 | Bring the sewing thread to the front at the tip of the shape and work a stitch into the padding.

8 | Work the last stitch across the padding to hold the ends in place.

9 | Complete the remainder of the padding in a similar manner.

169

PURLS OVER STRING PADDING

Purls are traditionally placed at a 45° angle over soft cotton padding. To achieve a good finish it is important that all the pieces of purl are cut accurately. If you are working a straight line, cut one purl and use this as a template for the remaining lengths. For tapered shapes, each piece must be measured and cut as the work progresses. Rotate your work so the line of padding is vertical. Use doubled, waxed sewing thread.

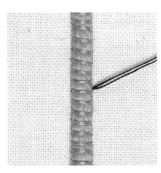

1 | Bring the thread to the front halfway along the padding, close to the right-hand side.

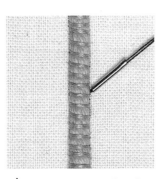

2 | Thread a length of purl onto the needle and gently slide it onto the fabric.

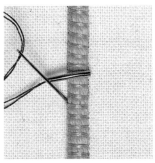

3 | Lay the purl across the padding at a 45° angle. Check the fit and adjust if necessary. Take the needle to the back on the opposite side, angling it slightly under the padding.

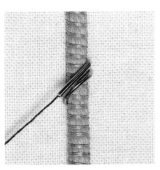

4 | Bring the thread to the front one purl's width above the first purl. Thread a second piece onto the needle. Slide it gently onto the fabric and lay it across the padding as before.

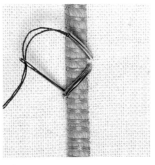

5 | Take the needle to the back close to the previous purl, angling it under the padding.

6 | Continue in this manner, taking a tiny back stitch close to the padding after every three or four purls to maintain a constant tension.

7 | To work the second half, rotate the work 180°. Bring the thread to the front on the right-hand side of the padding and take it to the back on the left-hand side.

ATTACHING PURL OVER PADDING

To maintain the correct angle, the stitches should be close together when the needle is taken to the back and spaced a purl's width away when it is brought to the front. The spacing of the stitches on the emerging side will be further apart than those on the entering side.

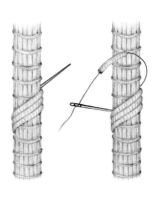

blackwell roundel

before you begin

We recommend that you read the complete article

See the liftout pattern for the embroidery design

All embroidery is worked with ONE strand of thread

this design uses

Back stitch / Beading / Cut purl
Chipping / Couching
Double back stitch (shadow work)
Double running stitch / Eyelet
Fly stitch / Linked eyelets
Long and short stitch
Pin stitch variation / Pleated plate
Satin stitch / Shadow appliqué
Split stitch / Whipping

The finished design measures 10cm (4") in diameter.

requirements

FABRIC

30cm x 60cm wide (12" x 24") piece of ivory silk organza

15cm x 30cm wide (6" x 12") piece of gold metallic silk dupion

SUPPLIES

4cm x 6cm wide (1½" x 2⅜") piece of mottled gold kid leather

6cm (2⅜") square of beige wool felt

10cm (4") embroidery hoop

20cm (8") embroidery hoop with both rings bound

Beeswax

Ball-tipped lace scissors (optional)

Goldwork scissors

Velvet cutting pad

Fine, short pins

Mellor

Dressmaker's awl or stiletto

Blunt-nose tweezers

Small paintbrush

Acid-free craft glue

4cm x 6cm wide (1½" x 2⅜") piece of light card

Tracing paper

Fine black pen

H mechanical pencil

NEEDLES

No. 12 bead embroidery

No. 8 crewel

No. 10 crewel

No. 12 crewel

No. 22 chenille

THREADS, BEADS & SEQUINS

Au ver à Soie, Soie 100/3
A = 102 ivory
B = 694 pale flesh

Au ver à Soie, soie d'Alger stranded silk
C = 2578 lt mocha
D = 3432 vy lt sable
E = 4143 lt mahogany
F = 4145 med mahogany

Au ver à Soie, soie perlée silk pearl
G = 634 beige

Devere 6 thread silk floss
H = 13 brown
I = 50 lily
J = 60 eggshell
K = 90 ingot
L = 166 biscuit

DMC floche
M = ecru

Fine silk gimp
N = brown–27cm (10½")
O = eggshell–30cm (12")
P = grey–27cm (10½")
Q = lily–10cm (4")
R = old gold–60cm (24")

Heavy rayon gimp
S = old gold–20cm (8")

Polyester sewing thread
T = beige

Silk sewing thread
U = old gold

Metal threads
V = copper super pearl purl–7cm (2¾")
W = very fine 2% gold pearl purl–68cm (27")
X = no. 10 2% gold smooth purl–4cm (1⅝")
Y = no. 8 bright check purl–5cm (2")
Z = eggshell silk covered plate–50cm (20")
AA = old gold bright check purl–15cm (6")
AB = dull copper smooth purl–10cm (4")
AC = old gold smooth purl–40cm (16")
AD = pale beige smooth purl–10cm (4")

BEADS

Glass pearls
AE = 2mm cream (40)
AF = 3mm cream (6)

Czech Charlotte no. 15 seed beads
AG = 24ct gold AB (50)
AH = brushed copper (120)

Miyuki no. 15 seed beads
AI = 1602 matte transparent beige (55)
AJ = 2196 lined topaz AB (16)

Miyuki no. 11 seed beads
AK = 592 antique ivory pearl Ceylon (30)

SEQUINS & PAILLETTES

AL = 3mm dull gold sequins (16)
AM = 2mm gold paillettes (16)

> **NOTE:** Metal threads are delicate, especially soft, 2% gold threads. Handle with care

preparation for embroidery

PREPARING THE FABRICS

Cut the silk organza in half so that you have two, 30cm (12") squares. Neaten the edges of the organza with a machine zigzag or overlock stitch. Cut the silk dupion in half so that you have two, 15cm (6") squares.

TRANSFERRING THE DESIGN

SILK ORGANZA

Using the black pen, trace the embroidery design onto tracing paper. Centre one organza square in the 20cm (8") hoop and carefully tension until the fabric is taut. Turn the hoop over and centre over the tracing with the fabric flat to the paper.

Using the mechanical pencil, lightly transfer the design lines to the organza. Replace the fabric in the hoop so that the pencil marks are uppermost. Ensure the surface is taut.

FELT PADDING

Trace the quince leaf, acorn cap and rose centre templates onto tracing paper with the black pen. When ready to use, cut out, leaving a small border around each template. Pin or tape the templates to the felt and cut out along the marked lines.

KID LEATHER

Trace the quince and rose leaves onto tracing paper with the black pen. When ready to use, cut out, leaving a small border around each template. Tape to the light card and cut out along the inside edge of the marked lines. Check that they fit the corresponding leaves on the design and adjust if necessary. Trace around the card templates on the wrong side of the kid leather and cut out.

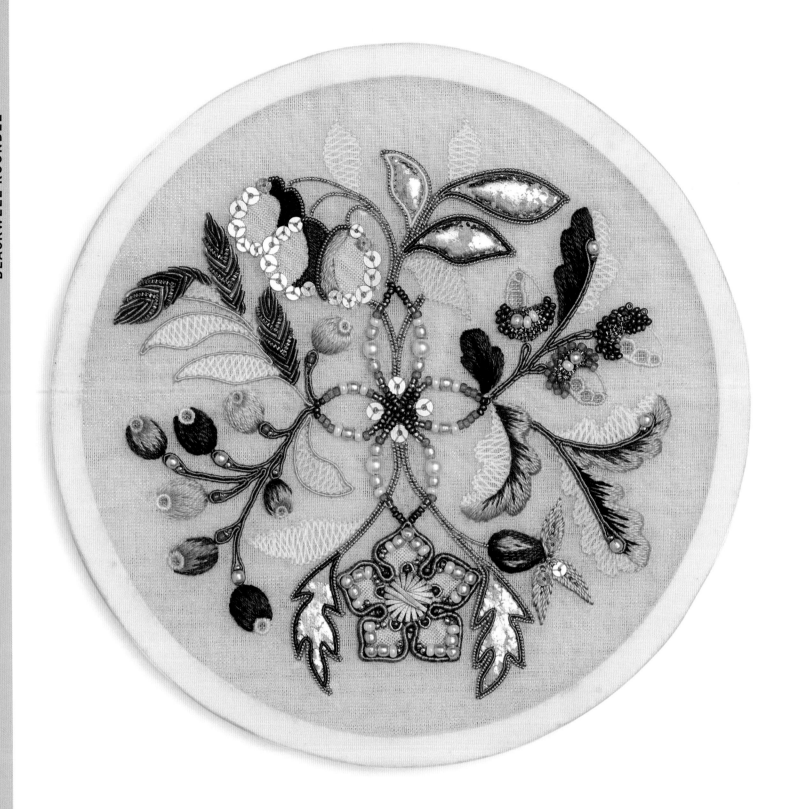

embroidery

See pages 180–181 for step-by-step instructions for working double back stitch and an eyelet.

Refer to the close-up photograph for colour and stitch placement.

Use the no. 8 crewel needle for the silk pearl, the no. 12 crewel for the kid leather and the no. 12 bead embroidery for attaching beads, sequins, paillettes, chips and cut purls. Use the no. 10 crewel needle for all remaining embroidery. The no. 22 chenille needle is used with a thread lasso to sink gimp thread tails to the wrong side of the work.

All embroidery is worked in the hoop.

ORDER OF WORK

SHADOW WORK

Embroider the rowan, oak and rose shadow work leaves with double back stitch using **A** or **B**.

Embroider one half of each oak leaf with double back stitch, taking care at the corners that the long stitch on the wrong side is kept within the outline.

SHADOW APPLIQUÉ

Rose

Place one of the gold dupion squares into the small hoop, ensuring the fabric is taut and the grain is straight. Position the hoop behind the design so that the dupion is flat against the wrong side of the organza and is centered behind the rose motif. Pin the hooped silk in place around the inner edge of the hoop.

Using **U**, embroider around the outer edge of the rose with pin stitch variation (diag 1).

> **PIN STITCH VARIATION:**
>
> Bring the thread to the front at A. Make a stitch between B and C. Work the next stitch from B back into the hem at D. The thread is pulled firmly at this step.
> Continue to the end of the line.

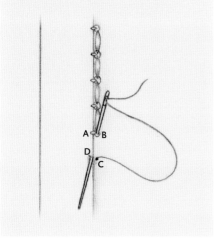

The stitches should be only 1mm (1/32") long. Work the pin stitch variation around the outer edges of the petals only, omitting the inner 'loop' between the petals (diag 2).

When the pin stitching is complete, remove the pins and turn the work to the wrong side. Carefully remove the small hoop. Trim the excess gold fabric to 2cm (3/4") from the stitching. Taking care not to pierce the organza, snip into the valley between petal tips. Holding the excess fabric with gentle tension, cut away the fabric right up against the pin stitching.

> **HINT: Ball-tipped lace scissors**
>
> Ball-tipped lace scissors are ideal to avoid piercing the organza with sharp scissor tips.
>
> If you don't have lace scissors, slide a strip of paper between the fabric layers to act as a shield over the organza.

Quince fruits

Apply the remaining square of gold silk dupion behind the fruits in the same manner as the rose, working pin stitch variation around the outer edges of the cluster. As you work, embroider back stitch along the outer edge of the centre and front fruits (diag 3).

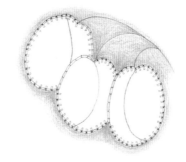

LAYERING THE FABRICS

A second layer of organza provides a stronger base for working the remaining embroidery.

Remove the work from the hoop. Place the remaining square of silk organza on a flat surface and position the embroidered organza on top, aligning the straight grain.

Place both fabrics into the embroidery hoop, carefully tensioning them until they are taut and lay smoothly together.

QUINCE FRUITS

Begin with the rear and centre fruits. Outline the right-hand section of the rear fruit with split stitch using **F**. Outline the right-hand section of the centre fruit with split stitch using **E**.

Using **F** and beginning at the upper edge, fill the outlined section of the rear fruit with angled satin stitch, working over the outline.

Fill the right-hand section of the centre fruit in a similar manner using **E**.

Outline the left-hand section of the front fruit with split stitch using **C**. Fill the shape with angled satin stitch using the same thread and working over the outlines.

Embellish sections of the fruit outlines as shown with **AL** and **AM** using a lightly waxed length of **T**. Use **AL** for the wider, centre section of a line and **AM** to taper the width at each end. Attach each sequin or paillette using three stitches.

QUINCE LEAVES

Cut out the leaf felt padding pieces. Centre one piece within the corresponding shape on the organza. Stab stitch in place using **T**, emerging on the design line and taking the needle to the back through the felt. Begin with stitches at key points around the shape to hold it accurately in position and fill in between. The stitches should be 1mm (1/32") long and half this length apart. Repeat for the remaining two leaves.

Cut the leaf shapes from the kid leather and apply over the felt padding, stab stitching them in place in the same manner as the felt. To prevent the leather tearing, take care not to stitch too close to the edge.

ROWAN BERRIES

Embroider the eyelets using **A** or **B**. Fill each berry with padded satin stitch using combinations of **C**, **D**, **E** and **F**, referring to the photograph for colour placement. Use

the main shade for a berry to work the outline with split stitch. Changing to **M**, work a layer of padding along the length of the berry, leaving a gap between the padding and the outline to allow for a second layer. Begin in the centre and work the stitches back and forth so that the padding is not replicated on the back (diag 4).

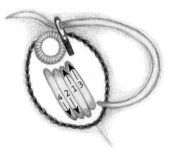

Add a second layer at an angle to the first. To end off the thread, run it under the padding stitches on the front of the work.

Cover the berry, including the outline, with satin stitch using the main thread colour and beginning at the centre of the shape. Angle the needle towards the centre stitch and hold it parallel to the split stitch outline.

Changing to a second colour as indicated, work stitches of varying lengths over the previous, emerging through the berry and taking the needle to the back at the outer edge.

OAK LEAVES

Fill the remaining half of each large leaf with padded satin stitch using combinations of **C**, **D**, **E** and **F**. Work the outer edge of each leaf half

with split stitch using the main colour. Fill with split stitch padding using **M**, keeping the stitches as long as possible. Split the stitches near the tip rather than the centre, keeping most of the thread on the surface and very little on the wrong side. Begin beside the vein and work back and forth along the length of the leaf to the outer edge.

Using the main colour, work satin stitch over the padding, including the outline.

Changing to a second colour, work stitches of irregular length over the previous stitching along the inner edge of the leaf half.

Outline the small oak leaf with split stitch using **E**. Beginning at the centre and using the same thread, work a row of long and short stitch from within the leaf to the upper edge. Changing to **F**, work a second row from within the previous stitching to the base.

ACORNS

Nut

Each nut is embroidered in the same manner. Beginning beside the acorn cap, outline the scalloped shape for the linked eyelets with double running stitch using **A** or **B**, keeping the stitches small. Use the awl or stiletto to pierce a hole in the organza, centred within the first scallop. Enlarge the hole to near the running stitch outline. Begin to overcast the eyelet edge from beside the acorn cap along the outer edge, taking the needle down through the centre and bringing it up through the fabric (diag 5).

When you reach the end of the first scallop shape, pierce the organza at the centre of the second scallop and open

the hole, keeping a fabric 'bridge' between the holes the same width as the overcast edge. Throw the thread to the opposite edge of the bridge and wrap back to the overcast edge (diag 6).

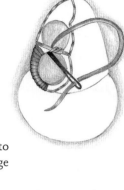

Continue to overcast the outer edge past the second eyelet towards the third scallop shape. When reaching the beginning of the third scallop, make a third hole and wrapped bridge in the same manner as before. Complete the overcasting around the outer edge of the linked eyelets.

Embroider the remaining nut outline with whipped back stitch using the same thread as the linked eyelets.

Caps

Cut out the cap felt padding pieces and attach to the organza in the same manner as before. Cut tiny chips from **Y**. The chips should be as long as they are wide and are attached in the same manner as beads.

Cover the felt padding with beads (**AE**, **AH**, **AI** and **AK**) and chips (**Y**) using a lightly waxed length of **T**. Position **AE** and **AK** beads at the centre, surround them with **Y** chips and attach **AH** or **AI** beads around the outer edge. Ensure the chips sit at different angles to one another for the best, sparkling effect.

ROSE

Centre

Cut out and attach the felt padding piece in the same manner as before. Fold and attach **Z** over the felt using a lightly waxed length of **T** in the following manner. Fold under 2mm (¹/₁₆") of **Z** at one end and pinch with the tweezers. Position the fold over the edge of the felt and work a stitch over the fold, in line with the felt edge, to hold the end of the plate in place (diag 7).

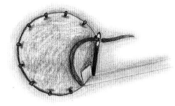

Lock the couching stitch in place by working a tiny stab stitch nearby through the felt. Lay the plate across the circle to the opposite edge. Work a couching stitch across the plate at the edge of the felt (diag 8).

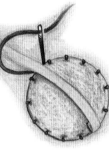

Maintain tension on the thread and fold the plate over the stitch. Work a locking stab stitch through the felt nearby.

Lay the plate across the circle to the opposite edge, crossing over the previous length, so that it lies beside the previous fold at the edge. Work a couching stitch over the plate at the edge of the felt, fold the plate and lock with a stab stitch as before.

Repeat this process, folding and couching the plate back and forth, until the circle is filled. All passes of plate should cross at the centre.

Hold the last length of plate with the tweezers, with the inner edge of the tweezers aligned with the edge of the circle. Twist the tweezers to fold the plate under. Remove the tweezers and pinch the fold. Trim the plate tail to 2mm (1/16"). Carefully couch the folded end in place at the edge of the felt. Secure the thread with two tiny back stitches along the edge of the nearest rose petal.

Petal outlines

Leaving a 2cm (3/4") tail, couch **S** around the petal outlines using **U**. Begin at the base of the flower between two petals. For a sharp point at a petal tip, emerge

slightly beyond the tip and take the needle to the back down through the gimp. Maintaining a firm tension on the thread, bend the gimp back on itself and pinch the fold with the tweezers. Work a locking stab stitch a little further along the next edge to be covered by the gimp.

Continue to couch the gimp along the petal edges as before. When reaching the beginning, cut the excess gimp, leaving a 2cm (3/4") tail.

Open a hole with the awl or stiletto and sink the tails using a lasso.

Carefully unravel the covering of the gimp tails, taking care not to unravel too far. Overcast the base of each tail for 5mm (3/16") along the nearby petal edges, one to each side. Trim away the excess gimp.

Using a lightly waxed length of **U**, embellish the petal edges inside the gimp outline with beads, attaching each one with a back stitch. Begin with an **AE** bead at the tip and add an **AE** bead at each side of the first. Add an **AK** bead at each side followed by two **AG** beads. Attach an **AH** bead at the centre base of each petal and inside the loop of gimp between the petals.

Surround each **AH** bead at the base of each petal with a loop of **X** using lightly waxed **U**. Cut five, 3mm (1/8") lengths of **X**. Emerge at the edge of the rose centre at one side of the bead. Thread on a length of cut purl and ease the purl down to the fabric. Take the needle to the back on the opposite side of the bead, pulling the thread through until the purl curves around the bead. Couch the centre of the loop, pulling the thread until it settles at the base between two coils.

HINT: Cutting smooth purl

Handle these delicate tubes of coiled metal with care. Cut pieces of purl are attached in the same manner as beads.

Use scissors reserved for cutting metal threads, and cut the purls over a small, velvet-covered pad or tray. The velvet catches the purls, and the smooth pile will not get caught up in the coils of the purl.

ROSE LEAVES

Cut the two rose leaves from the kid leather. Using the small paintbrush, coat the wrong side with a thin layer of glue. Position each leaf over the corresponding shape on the organza, press in place and leave to dry. Using **T**, work tiny stab stitches around the edges in the same manner as before, emerging through the fabric only at the edge of the shape and taking the needle to the back through the leather.

ROSE HIP

Outline the hip with split stitch using **E**. Changing to **M**, fill the shape with three layers of padding, working back and forth in the same manner as before. Work the final layer at an angle across the shape. Cover the shape with satin stitch using **E**, beginning at the centre and completing one side at a time. Work the two patches of highlight over the top of the previous stitching using **C** and add a few stitches using **F**.

Sepals

Beginning with a 3mm (1/8") straight stitch from the centre vein to the tip, embroider each sepal with fly stitch using **G**. Attach a paillette (**AM**) at the base of each sepal with three stitches using **T**.

QUINCE AND ROSE OUTLINES

Metal threads

Refer to the hints for couching pearl purl. Use lightly waxed lengths of **U** to couch all the pearl purl outlines.

Quince

Outline each kid leather leaf with **W**. Begin at the base of the lower leaf stem and couch to the base of the leaf.

Couch around the upper edge of the leaf, emerging at the edge of the kid, going over the pearl purl and to the back through the edge of the kid, angling the needle under the pearl purl. Emerge a little beyond the leaf tip and couch over the pearl purl. Maintaining tension on the thread, bend the pearl purl around the stitch with your finger. Pinch the bend with the tweezers to make the point sharper. Continue couching along the base of the leaf to the top of the stem.

Complete the stem with a second couched line of **W**. Outline the remaining quince kid leather leaves in the same manner.

Partially outline the quince fruits using **V**, couching in place using a lightly waxed length of **T**. Couch **W** along the fruit stems, beginning with the lower stem, followed by the upper and centre stems.

Using a lightly waxed length of **T**, attach four **AL** sequins at the centre of the design, ensuring space is left for the bead outlines.

Couch **W** along the 'Y' shaped stems connecting the quince to the centre of the design. Begin with the outer lines followed by the inner. The bead outlines will be worked over the pearl purl.

HINTS: Couching pearl purl

Before using a length of pearl purl, gently hold each end of the metal thread in your fingers. Carefully stretch the piece very slightly so that a tiny space opens between the coils. Do not overstretch.

Neaten one end by cutting away a few coils and place this end at the starting point for the couched line.

To couch the pearl purl, work the stitches in the same direction as the spiral of the purl, placing each stitch between two coils and pulling the thread down to disappear into the spiral.

At the beginning of the purl pearl, work two stitches between the first two coils and a single stitch between each of the next three. To continue, work a stitch between every two or three coils.

Work a locking stitch after each turn to secure the thread. Position these stitches along the design lines so they will be concealed by the metal thread.

When nearing the end of the line, trim the pearl purl so that it is slightly longer than needed. Cut away the excess length one coil at a time until it is the exact length required. Complete the couching with a stitch between each of the last few coils.

Rose

Outline the kid leather rose leaves in the same manner as the quince leaves. Begin beside the lower sequin at the centre of the design and work around each leaf from the outer edge to the inner, returning to the sequin.

Silk gimp

Leaving 2cm (¾") tails, couch a line of **N**, **P** or **Q** inside the pearl purl outlines of each kid leather leaf using a doubled length of **H**, **I** or **L** to match. Begin at the base of the leaf and couch at 2mm (¹⁄₁₆") intervals, emerging beside the pearl purl outline, taking the thread under and over the gimp, and angling the needle back under the metal thread. This ensures the gimp lies against the pearl purl.

Turn the gimp at the tip in a similar manner to the pearl purl outlines, without pinching the bend. Take the gimp tails to the back in the same manner as the rose petal outline.

BEAD OUTLINES

Work the bead outlines at the centre of the design with a couched string of beads using **AE**, **AF**, **AG**, **AH**, **AI**, **AJ** and **AK**.

Using a lightly waxed length of **R**, emerge at the inner point of the lower leaf shape and thread on beads for the first edge in the following order:

3 x **AH**	1 x **AE**	1 x **AI**
1 x **AG**	1 x **AF**	1 x **AJ**
1 x **AJ**	1 x **AE**	1 x **AG**
1 x **AI**	1 x **AK**	3 x **AH**

NOTE: The copper beads used in the original design were slightly smaller and the number of beads has been adjusted to fit the space.

Take the thread to the back at the tip of the shape. Pull through until the beads lie along the curve and work a locking stab stitch along the design line. Leave the thread at the tip.

Using a new waxed length of **T** couch over the line of beads at each side of the group of three pearl beads to anchor the curve. Beginning at the tip, couch between each bead back to the inner point.

Using the thread left at the tip, thread on the reverse combination of beads. Take the thread to the back at the inner point and couch the line of beads along the second edge in the same manner as before. Repeat for the upper leaf shape.

Couch beads along the edges of the remaining leaf shapes in a similar manner using beads in the following order:

2 x **AH**	1 x **AI**	1 x **AK**
1 x **AG**	1 x **AK**	2 x **AI**
1 x **AJ**	1 x **AE**	2 x **AH**

Reverse the order for the second edge as before.

ROWAN AND OAK STEMS

Embroider the stems with couched lines of **R** using **K** doubled in the needle. Begin and end with 2cm (¾") tails, taking them to the back in the same manner as before.

Rowan

Beginning at the base of the large stem, couch the lower line to the first berry. At the tip, turn the gimp forming a loop, working a locking stitch to help secure the curve. Continue couching back to the main stem and work a sharp bend in the same manner as the rose and quince leaf outlines. Continue couching the remainder of the stem outline with a loop at the base of each fruit and a sharp bend where needed at the base of a stem. Work the small stem separately. Attach two beads within each loop at the base of the berries, **AE** and **AG** or **AI** and **AG**, using lightly waxed **T**.

Oak

Embroider the couched gimp stems in the same manner as the rowan stems, making the loops at the base of the acorns a little smaller. Attach two beads, **AE** and **AG**, in the loops at the tips of the leaves in the same manner as before.

CUT PURL ROWAN LEAVES

Padding

Outline each leaf with split stitch using **M**. With the same thread work two layers of padding in the same manner as before, with the final layer along the length of the leaf.

Cut purl

Fill each leaf with cut purl work using **AA**, **AB**, **AC** and **AD**. Attach the cut purls in the same manner as beads with a doubled length of lightly waxed **U**. To attach each piece, emerge on the centre vein, thread on the cut purl, slide it down to the fabric and take the needle to the back at the edge of the leaf. Begin with a 4mm–5mm (³/₁₆") length of **AC** and secure over the centre vein so that the outer end extends a little beyond the leaf tip on the design (diag 9).

Measure and cut a second 4mm–5mm (³/₁₆") piece of **AC** to lie just below the centre piece. Angle the needle towards the tip of the design and slightly under the tip of the previous purl. Repeat above the first piece of purl. Complete the leaf in the same manner, adding cut

purls from side to side, incorporating **AA**, **AB** and **AD** as desired.

For the outer leaf, only add cut purls to the upper side for the last few pieces. To tuck the tip of these beneath the previous purl, measure, cut and thread on the purl piece as before. Gently lift the centre of the previous purl using the mellor. Angle the needle under the centre of the previous purl. Pull the thread through, bringing the new purl piece into position, and remove the mellor.

REMAINING OUTLINES

Couch **O** around the shadow work rowan leaves using a doubled length of **J** in the same manner as previous gimp outlines. Couch over the gimp towards the leaves, taking care not to conceal the line of double back stitch. Take the gimp tails to the back and secure in the same manner as before.

EYELETS

Before working an eyelet a hole must be opened in the fabric using an awl or stiletto. Take care to pierce the hole between the fabric threads, not through them.

1 | Mark a tiny circle on the fabric. Leaving a short tail, work a row of running stitches around the circle, leaving tiny stitches at the back.

2 | Work a split stitch through the first stitch in the circle, then bring the thread to the front just outside the outline at A.

3 | Trim the tail close to the fabric. Using an awl, pierce the fabric and open up the eyelet.

4 | Take the needle down through the hole and emerge on the outer edge. Pull the thread firmly.

5 | Continue working overcast stitches until two stitches from completing the circle. Work the final two stitches leaving them loose.

6 | Take the needle back through the two stitches and pull the thread until the loops sit firmly on the fabric. Snip the thread close to the stitching.

7 | Using the awl, re-pierce the eyelet from the front and back. This helps to settle the thread and fabric.

8 | Finished eyelet.

DOUBLE BACK STITCH

Double back stitch creates delicate shading within shapes on fine fabrics. Back stitches are worked alternately along each side of the shape, outlining it and forming herringbone stitch on the wrong side of the work. These long, criss-crossing stitches create a lace-like pattern that is visible through sheer and light fabrics. Keep the back stitches for the shadow work small and aligned along each side of the shape.

1 | Begin with a waste knot near the tip. Work two tiny back stitches at the start of one line.

2 | Work a back stitch from A to B, covering the two tiny back stitches.

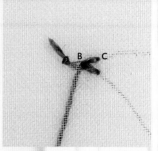

3 | Work a back stitch from C to B on the opposite side.

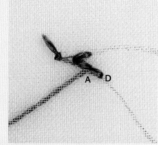

4 | Work a second back stitch along the first side from D to A.

5 | Repeat on the opposite side from E to C.

6 | Cut away the waste knot and thread tail from the wrong side after a few stitches.

7 | Continue to work back stitches, alternating from side to side along the shape.

8 | To work a curve make the stitches on the outer line longer and inner line shorter, to maintain alignment.

bee-eaters

before you begin

We recommend that you read the complete article

See the liftout pattern for the embroidery design

All embroidery is worked with ONE strand of thread

this design uses

Back stitch / Colonial knot
Long and short stitch / Split stitch
Straight stitch / Whipping

The finished design measures 15.5cm x 12cm wide (6⅛" x 4¾").

requirements

FABRIC

40cm x 35cm wide (16" x 14") piece of mushroom cotton sateen

40cm x 35cm wide (16" x 14") piece of quilter's muslin

SUPPLIES

25cm (10") embroidery hoop or stretcher bars to fit fabric

Thumbtacks (stretcher bars)

Tracing paper

Fine black pen

Fine heat-soluble fabric marker

NEEDLES

No. 10 crewel
No. 12 crewel

THREADS

Au ver à Soie, soie d'Alger stranded silk
A = F15 bright gold
B = 125 dk tropical blue
C = 131 ultra lt turquoise
D = 136 dk turquoise
E = 615 dk burnt orange
F = 1713 lt blue-grey
G = 1715 med blue-grey
H = 1716 dk blue-grey
I = 1723 teal
J = 1744 med Indian blue
K = 1745 dk Indian blue
L = 1746 vy dk Indian blue
M = 2133 olive green
N = 2134 med olive green
O = 2135 dk olive green
P = 2136 vy dk olive green
Q = 2522 vy lt gold
R = 2544 med corn
S = 2546 vy dk corn
T = 2614 med copper
U = 2615 dk copper
V = 2622 vy lt mahogany
W = 2625 med mahogany
X = 2636 dk terracotta
Y = 3423 sage
Z = 3716 dk grey-green
AA = 3722 vy lt pine green
AB = 4098 white
AC = 4104 champagne
AD = 4106 black

AE = 4223 lt golden tan
AF = 4224 golden tan
AG = 4241 vy lt tobacco
AH = 5022 lt sea green
AI = 5023 sea green

DMC stranded cotton
AJ = 169 lt pewter grey
AK = 310 black
AL = 317 pewter grey
AM = 535 lt charcoal
AN = 597 teal
AO = 598 lt teal
AP = 611 dk taupe
AQ = 613 lt taupe
AR = 646 dk beaver grey
AS = 727 lt golden yellow
AT = 743 yellow
AU = 920 med copper
AV = 928 vy lt grey-green
AW = 3021 vy dk Jacobean green
AX = 3371 black-brown
AY = 3781 dk French grey
AZ = 3799 vy dk pewter grey
BA = 3846 lt tropical blue
BB = 3856 vy lt mahogany
BC = 3865 winter white

Piper's Silks silk floss
BD = bright ocean
BE = grey
BF = mahogany
BG = stone
BH = burnt copper

preparation for embroidery

PREPARING THE FABRICS

Neaten the raw edges of the sateen and muslin with a machine zigzag or overlock stitch to prevent fraying.

TRANSFERRING THE DESIGN

Using the black pen, trace the embroidery design and placement marks onto the tracing paper. Using a light box or window, centre the sateen fabric over the tracing, ensuring the placement marks are aligned with the straight grain. Transfer the design using the heat-soluble fabric marker.

Aligning the edges, place the sateen, design side uppermost, over the piece of quilter's muslin. Mount the fabrics together in the hoop or frame tensioning until the surface is drum tight and ensuring that the grain remains straight.

If using a frame, begin at the centre of one long side, placing tacks at regular intervals at each side of the centre. Secure the opposite side, working from the centre to each end, followed by the two short sides.

> **HINT:** To help prevent snagging threads while stitching, push the tacks into the sides of the stretcher bars rather than the upper surface.

embroidery

Use the no. 10 crewel needle for the stranded silk and cotton and the no. 12 needle for the silk floss.

The following instructions list the colours used in each area but are not specific as to the positioning of each one. You will need to refer to the close-up photographs for colour placement.

All embroidery is worked in a hoop or frame.

ORDER OF WORK

All embroidery is worked in long and short stitch unless specified.

Tails

F, K, L, Y, Z, AA, AH, AI and **BF**

Outline the tail feathers with split stitch using **Z**.

Stitch the left-hand side of the large feather on **BIRD 1**, beginning on the outer edge with **L** and shading through **K, AI, Y** and **F**. Embroider the right-hand side using **F** and **Y**, adding **AA** at the outer edge. Stitch the tip with **L, Z** and **AI**. Work the centre vein in back stitch using **BF**.

Fill the small feather on the left-hand side with **F, L, Z, Y** and **AI**. Fill the small feather on the right-hand side with **G, Z** and **Y**.

Stitch the left-hand side of the large feather on **BIRD 2**, beginning on the outer edge with **Z** and shading through **Y** and **AH**. Embroider the right-hand side using **Y** and **AH**. Stitch the tip with **Z**. Embroider the upper section of the feather using **L, Y, Z** and **AI**. Work the centre line in back stitch using **BF** (fig 1).

Wing feathers

B, C, D, F, G, H, I, J, Y, AD, AM, AZ and **BF**

Stitch the feathers on **BIRD 1** using **B, F, G, I, J, Y** and **AH** (fig 2).

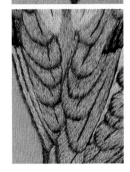

Embroider the feathers on **BIRD 2** using the same colours, omitting **B** and adding **C**.

Work the dark patches using **D, H, AD, AM** and **AZ** (fig 3).

Work the feather outlines with **G** and the centre lines in straight stitch using **BF**.

Branch

M, N, O, P, AP, AQ, AR, AW, AX and **AY**

Embroider the branch on the right-hand side of the design using **AP, AQ, AX** and **AY** and on the left-hand side using **AP, AQ, AR, AW, AX** and **AY**. On the left-hand side, whip some of the stitches and add colonial knots for texture using **AQ, AR** and **AY**. Stitch the leaves using **M, N, O** and **P**. Work the leaf stems with **N** and **AP** using straight stitch and whipping (fig 4).

Belly and breast

AN, AO, AV and **BG**

Beginning at the inner edge with **AN**, work the belly and breast on **BIRD 2**, shading through **AO** and **AV** and finishing on the outer edge with **BG**.

Side feathers

E, R, S, U, V, W, X, AA, AG and **BB**

Work the lower section of side feathers on **BIRD 2** using **E, V** and **BB** for the lighter areas and **U** and **W** for the darker areas (fig 5).

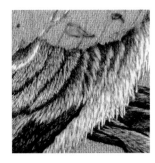

BIRD 1

BIRD 2

RK 2018

Stitch the upper section using **E**, **V** and **BB** for the lighter areas and **U**, **W**, **X** and **AG** for the darker areas (fig 6).

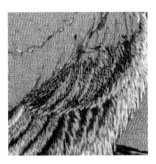

Add highlights using **AA** over the upper section.

Stitch the side feathers on BIRD 1 using **E**, **R**, **S**, **U**, **V**, **W**, **X** and **BB**.

Wing coverts and back

A, **Q**, **R**, **S**, **T**, **U**, **W**, **X**, **Y**, **AE**, **AF** and **AH**

Stitch the coverts working from the tips upwards using **Q**, **A**, **AE**, **AF**, **R**, **S** and **T** for the lighter areas and **U**, **W** and **X** for the darker areas (fig 7).

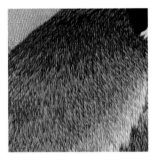

On BIRD 1, work the area between the coverts and down between the wings, beginning between the wings with **AH**, **Y** and **F** and blending up through **S** and **T** (fig 8).

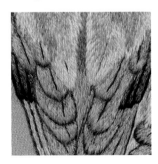

Head

R, **S**, **U**, **W**, **AB**, **AC**, **BA**, **BB**, **BD** and **BH**

Embroider the head on each bird, beginning at the upper back with the darker shades and working to the light using **U**, **W**, **S** and **R**.

Add angled straight stitches along the top head edge of BIRD 2 using **BH**.

Continue filling the head using **AC**, **AB**, **BB**, **BA** and **BD**.

Eye

AK, **AU**, **AX**, **BC** and **BE**

Stitch the pupil with split stitch using **AK**. Work a line of split stitch around the pupil using **BE**, then another line of split stitch using **AU**. Work a further line of split stitch using **BE** and surround this with a line of split stitch using **AX**. Embroider the highlight with a small straight stitch using **BC** (fig 9).

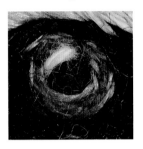

Eye band

AD, **AK**, **AX** and **BE**

Stitch the eye band using **AD** and **AK** on BIRD 1 and **AD**, **AK** and **AX** on BIRD 2. Add small straight stitch highlights under the eye using **BE** (fig 10).

Throat

C, **F**, **Q**, **R**, **AB**, **AC**, **AK**, **AS**, **AT**, **AV**, **BA**, **BC** and **BD**.

Work the throat on BIRD 1 using **C**, **F**, **Q**, **R**, **AB**, **AC**, **AK**, **AS**, **AT**, **AV**, **BA**, **BC** and **BD**. Stitch the throat on BIRD 2 in the same manner omitting **C**, **F**, **Q** and **AV** (fig 11).

Beak

AJ, **AL**, **AM**, **AW**, **AX**, **AZ** and **BE**.

Embroider the beak on BIRD 1 using **AX** for the nostril, **AZ**, **AM** and **AJ** for the upper beak and **AZ**, **AX** and **AM** for the lower beak (fig 12).

Stitch the beak on BIRD 2 using **AW** for the nostril, **AL** and **AJ** for the upper beak and **AZ** and **AX** for the lower beak (fig 13).

On both birds, stitch the dividing line between the upper and lower beak and the highlights with **BE**.

STITCH GLOSSARY

Back stitch

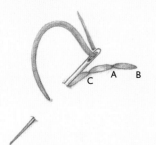

Beading

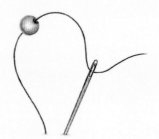

Blanket stitch

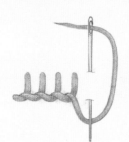

Blanket stitch bar

Chain stitch

Colonial knot

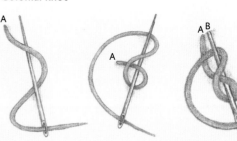

Coral stitch

Corded Coral stitch

Couching

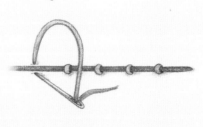

Cross stitch

Detached blanket stitch

Detached chain

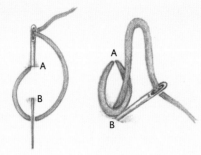

Double running stitch

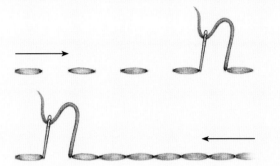

Fly stitch

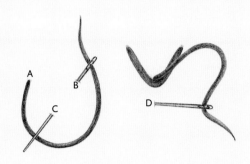

French knot

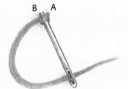

Heavy chain stitch

Leaf stitch

Long and short blanket stitch

Long and short stitch

Long-arm cross stitch

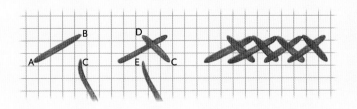

Outline stitch

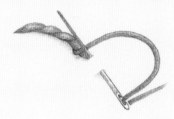

The thread is always kept above the needle

Overcasting

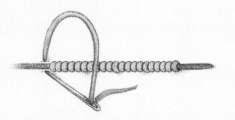

Padded satin stitch

satin stitch

chain stitch

seed stitch

Pistil stitch

Running stitch

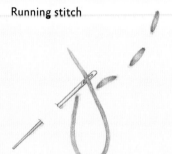

Satin stitch

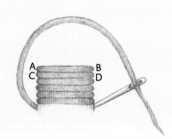

Seeding

Work as back stitches

Smyrna cross stitch

Split stitch

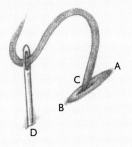

A
C
B
D

Stem stitch

The thread is always kept below the needle

Straight stitch

Tent stitch

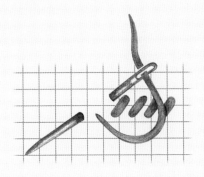

Trellis couching

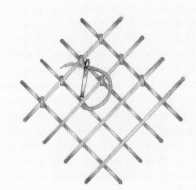

Up and down blanket stitch

Wheatear stitch

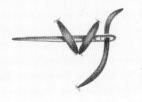

Woven spider web

CONTRIBUTORS

JENNY ADIN-CHRISTIE
Originally from Derbyshire, England, Jenny is a freelance professional hand embroiderer/designer, working to commission and inspiring others through enthusiastic teaching. She trained on the Royal School of Needlework's Intensive Apprenticeship, graduating with distinction in 1999, and has since worked on a broad range of commissions of national significance.

CHRISTINE P. BISHOP
Christine's love of embroidery and teaching has been a life-long journey and covers many styles from needlelace to surface stitchery and counted work. Through her extensive travels she has studied how things were done hundreds of years ago and developed usage of modern fabrics and threads making styles relevant to today.

HAZEL BLOMKAMP
Author of several books, Hazel has become well-known for her modern interpretation of crewel embroidery in which she uses a wide range of stitches and needlework techniques not normally associated with this style of stitching. She lives in South Africa and, apart from her books, has an extensive range of designs available on her website.

NICOLA JARVIS
An artist and professional hand embroiderer, Nicola trained at the Royal School of Needlework and received a Commendation from the Beryl Dean Award for Teaching Excellence in 2018. Her debut solo exhibition 'The Art of Embroidery: Nicola Jarvis and May Morris' was staged at the William Morris Gallery, London, in 2013 and in selected Arts and Crafts venues in the UK.

BARBARA KERSHAW
Born in England, Barbara now lives in Canada and has been teaching since 1997. With a passion for all forms of whitework but specializing in pulled thread, Italian-style drawn thread, Punto Antico, Casalguidi and Schwalm embroidery, Barbara loves to share her knowledge with anyone interested in learning.

JULIE KNIEDL
Julie's spectacular and innovative three-dimensional embroidery has featured in the pages of Inspirations publications from 2011 and her legacy continues since her passing in 2017. Using simple stitches, her elegant and realistic interpretations of natural subjects feature superb detailing and intricate workmanship.

RENETTE KUMM
Renette is passionate about stitching. Fascinated by fine silk embroidery, she studied different needlepainting techniques used all over the world. Fired by this inspiration, beautiful birds were the perfect subject matter to create her own magical needle art. Renette uses multiple colours to create magnificent portraits of her stunning subjects.

CATHERINE LAURENÇON
Catherine started needlepainting embroidery in 2001. Ten years later, in 2011, she obtained the prestigious title of "Meilleur Ouvrier de France" (Best Craftsman of France) which recognises the quality of her technique, the creativity of her designs and her inventive use of colour. She teaches needlepainting embroidery at home and abroad.

ANA MALLAH
A self-taught artist, Ana draws inspiration from anything pretty and flowers always seem to capture her interest the most. Passionate about embroidery, she particularly loves threadpainting and stumpwork. Ana works as an embroidery designer and teacher, and loves discussing stitches, threads and colours with like-minded people all day long.

BETSY MORGAN
Betsy has dabbled in every kind of needlework imaginable, but her first loves are counted thread and stumpwork. She has been designing and teaching needlework for 17 years and holds a fine arts degree in graphic design. Now living in the Charleston, South Carolina area, Betsy enjoys sharing in the stitching community there.

SUSAN O'CONNOR
Susan has devoted many years to exploring the world of embroidery. She has become renowned for her glorious botanical designs inspired by the Elizabethan period, worked with lustrous silk threads and gold paillettes. Susan teaches internationally, has authored two books and is the Editor of Inspirations magazine.

PHILLIPA TURNBULL
Phillipa has been producing beautiful embroidery kits for over 25 years. Her designs are based on the original crewel work she finds in the British castles and country houses that she has spent her career researching. Phillipa and her daughter, Arts and Crafts specialist Laura Turnbull, own and run The Crewel Work Company and Lady Anne's Needlework Retreats together.

KITS

FLOWER POTS
Page 84 Gorgeous trinket pots embellished with exquisite stumpwork flowers
Hydrangea kit contains: Fabrics, felts, wadding, wire, ribbon, card, template plastic, beads, embroidery threads and needles
Rose kit contains: Fabrics, felt, wadding, wire, cord, card, template plastic, embroidery threads and needles

JACOBEAN HUNT
Page 94 Magnificent crewel design filled with dynamic motifs
Kit contains: Pre-printed fabric, embroidery threads and needles

RED CURRANTS
Page 104 Luscious three-dimensional berries and leaves worked with fine, wool threads
Kit contains: Fabric, wire, beads, embroidery threads and needle

LE MAGNOLIA
Page 110 Stunning threadpainted magnolia worked in vibrant colours on linen
Kit contains: Fabric, embroidery threads and needle

VERSAILLES CHATELAINE
Page 114 Elegant silk needlebook with a monogram, pinwheel, scissor sheath and fob
Kit contains: Fabrics, mother-of-pearl rings and buckle, pins, ribbon, card, wadding, bead, paillettes, embroidery threads and needles

RETICELLA SAMPLER
Page 120 Italian cutwork needlelace designs from the 14th and 15th centuries
Kit contains: Fabric, embroidery threads and needles

WINTER SUNSET
Page 130 Glorious surface embroidery with gentle colours and textures
Kit contains: Fabrics, braid, embroidery threads and needles

LEAPING HARE
Page 142 Pretty linen sachet with a leaping hare worked in Casalguidi embroidery
Kit contains: Fabric, embroidery thread and needles

EDINBURGH ETUI
Page 152 Charming etui and accessories with counted work and surface embroidery
Kit contains: Fabrics, interfacings, interlining, polyester film, fibre-fill, card, felt, beading thread, beads, wooden thistle, embroidery threads and needles

THE LINNET
Page 164 Enchanting silk and goldwork bird, adorned with a sparkling crown
Kit contains: Fabric, metal threads, embroidery threads, beads and needles

BLACKWELL ROUNDEL
Page 172 Graceful Arts and Crafts inspired motifs in a range of techniques using silk and metal threads
Kit contains: Fabrics, felt, kid leather, metal threads, gimp, embroidery threads, beads, paillettes and needles

BEE-EATERS
Page 182 Superb threadpainted study of European bee-eaters
Kit contains: Fabric, embroidery threads and needles

THANK YOU.

Thank you to you, our passionate, loyal and amazingly talented readers. It is our privilege and joy to serve the needlework community.

This book is for you. To show off the craft you love and elevate the status of needlework to the platform it thoroughly deserves – the world's best.

This book has been hand-crafted by two groups of people:

The Designers.

To Ana, Barbara, Betsy, Catherine, Christine, Hazel, Jenny, Julie, Nicola, Phillipa, Renette and Susan, you are truly remarkable and gifted artisans – we are so grateful you have passion for the needle. Thank you for creating the gorgeous projects within this book; it is an honour to showcase your work and without you, these pages would be blank.

The Inspirations Team.

Susan & Ellaine – Thank you for curating, editing, proofing, creating the illustrations, stitching the step-by-steps, writing the words and showing the non-stitchers among us 'the way'.

Brendan, Natalie & Fiona – Thank you for finding Factoria VII, for creating the stunning environments for the projects to shine, and for taking some of the world's most beautiful photos of the world's most beautiful needlework.

Jessie, Sue & Lynton – Thank you for being an anchor, for finding the unfindable, for believing in this project and bringing it to life. You are the people behind the curtain – you make the magic happen.

Special Thanks.

Special thanks to Factoria VII for creating such an extraordinary location to shoot at, to Madeleine Fleming for being our glimpse of humanity, to Steve Evans for helping us wet our eyes and to Peter Kniedl for allowing Julie's legacy to live on.

Kristian & Andrea Fleming